PARLIAMENT
AND
INFORMATION

THE HOUSES OF PARLIAMENT
Plan of the Principal Floor

N

0   50   100   150 ft

OLD PALACE YARD

NEW PALACE YARD

STATUE OF CROMWELL

STATUE OF RICHARD I

ROYAL ENTRANCE

VICTORIA TOWER

NORMAN PORCH

QUEEN'S ROBING ROOM

ROYAL GALLERY

ROYAL COURT

CHANCELLOR'S GATE

PEERS' ENTRANCE

CHANCELLOR'S COURT

CHAIRMAN OF COMMITTEES

CLERK OF THE PARLIAMENTS

MINISTERS' ROOMS

STATE OFFICERS' COURT BDG

STATE OFFICERS' COURT

HOUSE OF LORDS

PRINCE'S CHAMBER

PEERS' COURT

BISHOPS CORRIDOR

PEERS' LIBRARY

PEERS' GUEST ROOM

PEERS' DINING ROOM

PEERS' DINING ROOM

LAW LORDS' CORRIDOR

PEERS' DINING ROOM

PEERS' LOBBY

PEERS' INNER COURT

KITCHEN

LOWER WAITING HALL

LOUNGE

STRANGERS' DINING ROOM

MEMBERS' DINING ROOM

CHESS ROOM

MEMBERS' SMOKING ROOM

BLACK ROD

OPPOSITION

MOSES ROOM

ST STEPHEN'S COURT

ST STEPHEN'S HALL

CENTRAL LOBBY

PEERS' CORRIDOR

COMMONS CORRIDOR

WHIPS

WHIPS

COMMONS INNER COURT

COMMONS LOBBY

ST STEPHEN'S ENTRANCE

ST STEPHEN'S PORCH

SERJEANT AT ARMS' OFFICES

CLOISTER COURT

WESTMINSTER HALL

GRAND COMMITTEE ROOM

CPA OFFICES

STAR COURT BDG

STAR CHAMBER COURT

AYE

NO

HOUSE OF COMMONS

COMMONS COURT

MEMBERS' TEA ROOM

COMMONS LIBRARY

MEMBERS' ENTRANCE

MINISTERS' ROOMS

CLERK OF THE HOUSE

CLOCK TOWER

SPEAKER'S COURT

SPEAKER'S GREEN

SERJEANT AT ARMS' RESIDENCE

SPEAKER'S RESIDENCE

SPEAKER'S RESIDENCE

TERRACE

RIVER THAMES

VICTORIA TOWER GARDEN

LORD CHANCELLOR'S DEPARTMENT

PARLIAMENT
AND
INFORMATION

The Westminster Scene

Dermot Englefield

Deputy Librarian
House of Commons, Westminster

© Library Association Publishing 1981. Published by Library
Association Publishing, 7 Ridgmount Street, London WC1E 7AE
and printed in Great Britain for the publishers by the Pitman Press,
Bath.

First published 1981

British Library Cataloguing in Publication Data

Englefield, Dermot J T
  Parliament and information
  1. Great Britain. Parliament
  I. Title II. Library Association
  328.41   JN550

  ISBN 0 85365 570 7 (Casebound)
  ISBN 0 85365 993 1 (Paperback)

*To my patient family
Dora, Gregory and Anna*

Designed by Ron Jones

Typeset by Lindonprint, Cambridge.
Printed and bound in Great Britain
at The Pitman Press, Bath

Contents

Plans and Illustrations

I would like to thank Sir Noel Short, Mr Speaker's secretary, for permission to use item 2; Mr K.R. Mackenzie for item 1; Dr Menhennet for item 3; Mr Peter Heaton for item 4; Mr Roger Morgan and HMSO for item 5; Mr M. Bond for item 6. I would like to thank Times Newspapers for permission to use Tables 1.1 and 1.2 and my colleague Trevor Haclin for permission to use his photograph on the cover.

Tables and Figures

Acknowledgements

While writing this book, I celebrated 25 years at the House of Commons. It provided a chance to tidy up my experiences and reflect on the general direction that Parliament has taken with regard to the question of information during the last quarter century.

It would have been impossible to do this without the unstinted help of colleagues and friends of long standing. This included a happy co-operation with colleagues in the House of Lords. I would like to thank Sir Peter Henderson, Clerk of the Parliaments and Sir Richard Barlas, former Clerk of the House of Commons. To these I would like to add Frank Allen, Clerk of the Journals in the House of Commons, and Maurice Bond, Principal Clerk, Information Services in the House of Lords. Other staff of the Lords who have helped me include Jeremy Maule, Information Clerk, Harry Cobb, Deputy Clerk of the Records, and Roger Morgan, once a colleague in the House of Commons Library, now Librarian of the House of Lords. In the House of Commons I would like to thank Michael Ryle, Clerk of Select Committees, Victor Le Fanu, Assistant Serjeant at Arms, and Roy Russell, Deliverer of the Vote, together with the whole staff of the Library itself who have, often unwittingly, helped me by challenging present ideas while still meeting present deadlines.

Finally I would like to thank the three Librarians I have worked with: Strathearn Gordon 1950–67, David Holland 1967–76, and David Menhennet 1976–   They are three quite different personalities who have each contributed something distinctive and important to the development of the House of Commons Library since the War and have also laced my time at the House of Commons with challenge and appreciation.

CRYSTAL PALACE, *June 1980*

Introduction

For centuries, Parliament has been at the centre of the nation's information network. Members of Parliament have drawn rein under the shadow of Westminster Hall with news and problems from their constituencies, Peers have descended from their carriages in Old Palace Yard straight from informed dinner parties; and today Ministers are whisked there in official black cars having flown in from international conferences, all returning to Westminster to contribute their grain of truth and prejudice to the great debate. Facts, ideas and feelings have been drawn into the political vortex and, with the help of its strict procedures, Parliament has shaped this information into Statutes and Resolutions, or approved Statutory Instruments and Reports which it has then sent back to the people to help shape our society. Yes, Parliament has always been in the information business even if today there are other centres of information such as the Civil Service.

Throughout these centuries, Parliament has been very sensitive to changes in its role. Any institution that has survived seven hundred years needs to be! In the seventeenth century there were struggles with the Crown, and then for two or three hundred years imperial themes and problems abroad, and great social change at home. In our own time with universal suffrage, Parliament has worried about the growth of bureaucracy, both its cost and its danger to the citizen's rights. In the session 1977–8 a Bill went through Parliament for direct elections to the European Parliament, a change which means that Parliament is set in a new institutional pattern. The fact that it is necessary to bring out every few years a new edition of Erskine May's *Parliamentary Practice*, a huge and detailed guide to Parliament's method of working, prepared under the editorship of the Clerk of the House of Commons, shows not only the pressures of these changes on Parliament, but also its responsiveness to them.

Maybe the most permeating of these changes in recent years and certainly one which affects not only Parliament but its Members as individuals, might go under the cryptic label 'the communications revolution'. It is not just that as government spreads further through our lives Members are required to grapple with problems over an ever-widening area, from the highly technical, through the human to the ethical; it is also the ever-increasing speed of response that is required of them.

It is a Thursday afternoon and a White Paper has come out on a subject which concerns Scotland. BBC Scotland (Glasgow) telephones one of the Members for Glasgow at Westminster, checks that he is flying to Scotland on an evening 'plane and asks him to appear on the 10.30 p.m. programme to comment on the Government's views, together with a political opponent. They will meet him at the airport and drive him direct to the studio. Here are the ingredients of the 'communications revolution' with the telephone, the 'plane, the car and finally the broadcasting medium, all comparatively recent inventions, all making possible, maybe necessary, an instant and informed response, a situation that would have bewildered Members of the age of the Pallisers.

Parliament and Information is being written a generation after the end of the Second World War. During that period, and especially in recent years there have been, within the Palace of Westminster, really significant changes in the staffing and the type of services afforded to Members to help them face their new challenges.

In the House of Lords the Parliament Office (as the department of officials serving it is known) was examined a few years ago and reshaped to include a new office, grouping some established tasks with some new responsibilities under a new Principal Clerk, Information Services. In the House of Commons in 1967 the Library ceased to be an office in the Speaker's Department and became a Department of the House in its own right. Since then there have been further reviews of the administration of the House of Commons, the most recent by a Select Committee under Mr Arthur Bottomley and significant changes are likely to spring from its recommendations. These are structural changes which acknowledge and respond to broad new needs, but in connection with Parliament and information there has been a long list of specific innovations and improvements which belies any view that the Palace of Westminster remains as nineteenth-century as its silhouette.

In the House of Lords the Record Office with its superb archive of Parliamentary Records has been air-conditioned, reorganized and equipped to the highest professional standards, a job which took nearly a quarter of a century. It was the House of Lords too that first introduced an official information point for enquiries from the public. Again it was the House of Lords that first introduced a regular computer-based information service for Parliament, although the House of Commons Library had conducted successful trials nearly a decade earlier. And it is the House of Lords Record Office which acts as guardian of the tapes of the newly started broadcasting of debates. In the session 1976–7, the House of Lords Library was carefully examined for the first time in 150 years and, under its new Librarian, has replaced historic treasures, such as the death warrant of Charles I and the Petition of Right in one of its principal rooms, with a microfilm reader/printer and a computer terminal.

In the House of Commons the Select Committees have been strengthened by the appointment of Specialist Advisors. The Library has expanded from a staff of six in 1946 to some 100 in 1980. The Commons too have designated a small information office for the public in the Library Department and appointed an

Education Officer who is to help students of Parliament of all ages. Members have called for a weekly supplement of House of Commons information to be published both for themselves and also for the general public. The House has also instructed the Library to computerize its elaborate indexing system so as to make it both more widely available and flexible to use. A Select Committee has examined the question of research assistants for Members and has recommended a doubling of the Research Division in the Library. These are some of the developments and proposals of recent years together with the addition of well over 150 personal assistants to help Members with their information needs.

Members of Parliament are busy men and for the most part they are not rich. It is for this reason that compared with the period before 1945 information services for Parliament have become much more institutionalized and, of course, more expensive. Yet compared with many similar or smaller countries – Germany, Canada, France and Australia for instance – the information support afforded to Peers and Members at Westminster is very modest and many, including the Library Association, have campaigned for more.[1,2] With great self-restraint Parliament moves slowly forward.

The best and fullest account of the network of information within which Members work is *The Member of Parliament and his Information* by A Barker and M Rush, (1970), which covers a wide spectrum, including constituency work, local government contacts, the role of the lobbies and the political parties etc., all of which lies outside Westminster itself. This work is confined to an account of Westminster which it is hoped may be of some help not only to library students and librarians, but also to others whose work or interests brings them into touch with the Houses of Parliament.

The book is arranged in two parts.

Part I, Information for Parliament, starts with the House of Commons and a brief account of its Members, their permanent staff, its work and the papers which are needed and produced. Against this background there follows a description of the work of the House of Commons Library. The House of Lords is then described in a similar way, including an account of the House of Lords Library but at much shorter length. Topics which are common to both Houses, including Statutes and Statutory Instruments, European Community Affairs, Parliamentary Records and a note on the use of computers at Westminster, are then examined. Mention is also made of the important work of Select Committees.

Part II, Information from Parliament, looks at Westminster from the outside and describes methods of obtaining information about Parliament and its work. Apart from offices in the Palace of Westminster itself, mention is also made of the media which are based there to provide a link between Parliament and the public. Finally, there are a number of appendices designed to be of use to reference librarians and others who need to know about Parliament and its documentation. This is brought together to form a small 'reference service'.

We elect a House of Commons because we believe our society needs certain policies and the Government which is subsequently formed attempts to carry them through. In time the House of Commons is dissolved and Members return to the electors to request a further term. It is this continuous dialogue between the public and Parliament through which our society maintains a certain freedom of political choice, and hence of social priorities, that makes the subject of 'Parliament and Information' a perennially interesting and important one, not least for those of us who work there.

Notes

1 *Library Association Record,* **63** (7) July 1961, pp.229-30.
2 *Second Report of the Estimates Committee* 1960-1 (168), V, pp.274-90.

PART I
Information for Parliament

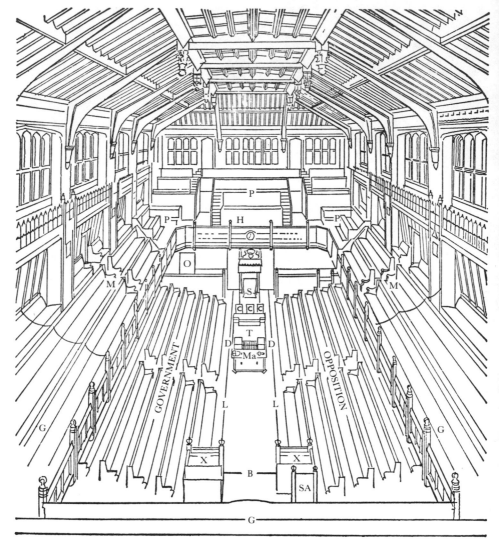

From a drawing by John Mansbridge

The Chamber of the House of Commons

KEY: S – Mr. Speaker. P – Press Galleries. H – *Hansard* Reporters. O – Government Officials' Box. C – Clerks of the House (when the House goes into Committee, Mr. Speaker leaves the Chair, and the Chairman sits in the chair of the Clerk of the House, which is the one on the left). T – Table of the House. D – Despatch Boxes. Ma – Mace (when the House goes into Committee, the Mace is put 'below the Table' on brackets). L – Lines over which Members may not step when speaking from the front benches. B – Bar of the House. X – Cross Benches. SA – Serjeant at Arms. M – Members' Galleries. G – Visitors' Galleries.

CHAPTER ONE

House of Commons

The Organization

MEMBERS

The 635 Members of Parliament who represent us are elected by a simple majority vote within individual constituencies. The average size of a constituency is about 65 000 voters. To vote you must be on the register of voters published the February before the election and to register you must be a citizen of the United Kingdom and aged 18. To stand as a candidate you must similarly be a citizen of the United Kingdom and aged 18 and you must put down a deposit of £150, which you lose if you do not secure 12½ per cent of the votes cast.

The Members who arrive at Westminster are a mixture of young and old, generalist and specialist, ambitious and idealistic. Their educational attainments are well above average as Table 1.1 shows.

Table 1.1 Educational background of MPs elected May 1979

	Lab	Cons	Lib	Other
Elementary and Secondary	112	13	–	5
Grammar School	108	90	4	5
Eton	1	50	1	–
Harrow	–	9	–	–
Other Public Schools	20	145	4	2
Service Colleges	–	16	–	–
Technical Colleges etc.	56	27	2	1
Oxford	38	94	2	–
Cambridge	20	75	1	1

Source: Times Guide to the House of Commons, May 1979, p.276

In May 1979 about 67 per cent of Members were university graduates. Members' specialist backgrounds cover a broad area as Table 1.2 suggests. In addition, most Members have expertise in a narrower area, together with very varied experience.

When they arrive at Westminster, Members are given a room or if not a room

Table 1.2 Professional and specialist backgrounds of MPs elected May 1979

	Cons	Lab	Lib	Others
Barristers and advocates	54	21	–	1
Solicitors	16	10	–	1
Journalists and authors	31	19	1	1
Publishers	5	–	–	–
Public relations	2	–	–	–
Teachers, lecturers	14	53	3	4
Doctors, surgeons, dentists	3	5	–	–
Farmers, landowners	25	2	2	1
Company directors	82	1	2	–
Accountants	12	4	1	–
Underwriters and brokers	17	–	–	–
Managers, executives and administrators	52	33	–	2
Architects and surveyors	5	1	1	–
Scientists	1	5	–	–
Economists	8	9	–	1
Banking	12	–	–	–
Diplomatic	2	1	–	–
Social Workers	1	3	–	–
Civil servants	–	3	–	–
Local government	1	2	–	–
Clerical and technical	1	3	–	–
Engineers	8	30	1	–
Mineworkers	–	16	–	–
Rail workers	–	9	–	–
Other manual workers	–	7	–	2
Trade union officials	1	27	–	–
Party officials	12	5	–	–
Hoteliers and publicans	–	–	–	2
Other business and professions	10	5	–	–
Ministers of religion	–	–	–	2

Source: Times Guide to the House of Commons, May 1979, p.276

at least a desk, filing cabinets, a locker near the chamber for their papers and will be reimbursed up to £6,750 p.a.[1] to pay for secretarial and personal research assistance, as they see fit. They also find that they control their conditions of work (not their pay and allowances) through a group of nineteen Members, chaired by the Leader of the House, known as the House of Commons (Services) Committee. The services referred to are those which support the working of the House and the Committee has four Sub-Committees covering Accommodation and Administration, Catering, the Library and, most recently, Computers.

STAFF

The staff of the House of Commons who support the 635 Members are slightly less numerous than the Members themselves, about 600. Their numbers have grown considerably in recent years as in 1964, for instance, they numbered only 278.

This staff service the House under Commissioners, set up under the House of Commons Administration Act 1978, who consist of the Speaker (Chairman), the Leader of the House, a Member of the House of Commons nominated by the Leader of the Opposition, and three other Members of the House of Commons who are not Ministers. These Commissioners are the employers of the staff and prepare estimates for the running of the House. The point of view of Members themselves is expressed to the Commissioners through the Services Committee.

The staff of the House of Commons is organized in five Departments[2]: the Clerk's Department, the Serjeant at Arms' Department, the Library Department, the Administration Department, and the Department of the Official Report of the House of Commons. All these Departments are involved in different ways in transmitting information to and from the House of Commons.

The Administration Department consists of the Fees Office, which deals with pay, allowances, etc., for Members and staff, and the Establishments Office which deals with staff matters for the whole House of Commons. The other four Departments are explained by their name, with the Clerk's Department providing procedural advice and assistance for the House, its Committees and Members individually; the Serjeant at Arms' Department running services such as accommodation, communications, security, etc., and the Library Department providing information and research services – excluding procedural questions which are undertaken by the Clerk's Department. The Department of the Official Report is responsible for reporting the debates which take place in the Chamber and in Standing Committees. Although the Departments are separate, from 1 January 1979 a Board of Management consisting of the Heads of all the Departments works together to run the services of the House of Commons, as directed by the new Commissioners.

WORK

The House of Commons sits about 36 weeks a year with the session often starting in early November. The daily sittings of the House start at 2.30 p.m. Mondays to Thursdays and 9.30 a.m. on Fridays. The sittings often continue until after midnight on Mondays to Thursdays and until 3 p.m. or later on Fridays. The House of Commons spends most of its time, following Question Time on Mondays to Thursdays which ends about 3.30 p.m. and throughout Friday, when there is no Question Time, discussing three different areas. First, there is legislation to be debated, the various stages of Bills. Secondly, there is the House's deliberative function, which embraces debate on the whole range of matters, both general and specific, whether of long-term importance or of an urgent character, for which the Government are currently responsible to the House. In this connection, documents printed by order of the House, as well as the publications of Government Departments, often form an essential element in the House's discussions. Thirdly – and constitutionally most important – is the House's control of finance, expressed through Budget debates and Finance Bills and through the Estimates for the public service.

The papers pertaining to this work of the House are the 'Vote' (to be described later), and sometimes Bills, Accounts and Papers or Command Papers, depending on the business. The record of what is *done* appears in the daily Votes and Proceedings and in the sessional volumes of the *Journal*. The record of what is *said* appears in *Hansard* the next day.

Much of the work of the House is undertaken in Committees and Sub-committees of Members, which may number as few as four Members and as many as 50. Committees are either Standing Committees, which consider legislation and occasionally other matters, or Select Committees, which have a running remit or a specific remit to consider particular subjects. Standing Committees commence early each session and are lettered A, B, C, etc., and in a session when there is a lot of legislation they may reach the letter H or K. On average they have 16-20 Members and once a Standing Committee has completed work on one Bill, which may involve ten or twenty sittings, and has reported the Bill back to the House, it will often be allotted another Bill, normally quite unrelated to the work it has been doing. There is no attempt for particular Standing Committees to specialize. The actual work of these Standing Committees is to go through the Bill clause by clause with the Minister explaining the proposals and to consider amendments and new clauses in order to improve the Bill. The papers pertaining to this work of the House, the work of Standing Committees, are the notices of amendments which form part of the 'Vote' and, of course, the Bill itself. The record of what is *done* by the Standing Committee is published as Minutes of Proceedings of Standing Committee A, B, C, etc. The record of what is *said* in Standing Committee appears as Standing Committee Debates in the same format as *Hansard* and nearly as quickly. For the most part Standing Committees meet at 10.30 a.m. and work through to about 1 p.m., and they are open to the public. A particular Committee meets twice or more a week and most Standing Committee meetings take place on Tuesday, Wednesday and Thursday mornings and afternoons, if necessary.

In addition to the lettered Standing Committees mentioned above, used to examine Bills, there is a First Scottish Standing Committee and a Second Scottish Standing Committee which consider Scottish legislation, a Scottish and Welsh Grand Committee which debates certain Scottish and Welsh affairs and, since the suspension of the Northern Ireland Parliament, a Northern Ireland Committee which debates Northern Ireland questions.[3] There is also a Regional Affairs Committee which meets occasionally on matters concerning the English regions. The House of Commons also appoints Standing Committees to debate certain Statutory Instruments and other similar documents. The debates of all these Committees are reported in the same Hansard format as the lettered Standing Committee debates. For details of publication of the debates of the House of Commons and its Standing Committees see under Parliamentary Debates below.

The second type of Committee is the Select Committee which is set up by the House to consider particular subjects. Select Committees may be set up for a Parliament such as the Services Committee, others are set up just for the session. Select Committees work by inviting written evidence, summoning and questioning witnesses and, after sifting the evidence, they draw up a report and present it to the House together with any recommendations they may make. Select Committees meet mostly at Westminster at different times of the day and evening and sometimes their meetings are in private. Certainly all their deliberations and their work on their report is in private. The papers pertaining to this work of the House include the evidence, if the Committee decides to print it, i.e. the oral evidence, sometimes published day by day and the written evidence, often published some time after the report to the House. In addition to this evidence there is the report which the House of Commons prints as a House of Commons Paper. The work of these Committees also features in the 'Vote' (to be described later).

In this section, I have tried to set down in summary form an outline of the House of Commons, its permanent staff and the bare bones of how it works as a background to a short account of its papers.

The Papers

THE VOTE

Each night there is printed by the St Stephen's Parliamentary Press and each morning there is distributed to Members and others by the staff of the Vote Office, a set of working papers known as the 'Vote'. These papers are in several series and, as has been already indicated, concern the work of the House, including the work done in Standing Committees and in Select Committees. The material for the 'Vote' is prepared by the Clerk's Department and in recent years has amounted to twenty or more bulky volumes a session. The text of the 'Vote' printed on white paper refers to business in the House on the day of issue or in the past, and text printed on blue paper refers to business for the future. As arranged in the House of Commons Library they are set out in Table 1.3.

For most practical purposes much of the 'Vote' is really only of current interest, although for researchers the papers can be crucial, giving as they do the actual detailed parliamentary history. They are the authoritative record so that a list of voters in a Division List is the official record of the result not the list which has been printed in *Hansard*. The 'Vote' is also the authority for various statistics on the working of the House, such as the time of sitting, the actual text of motions and the record of papers which have been laid before the House. Part of the 'Vote', namely the Votes and Proceedings, forms the basis of the *House of Commons Journal*. In short, though a complicated and unindexed publication, the 'Vote' is a vital part of information for the House of Commons and from the House of Commons.

Table 1.3 House of Commons 'Vote' as arranged in the Library

Title	Paper Colour	Pagination	Contents
1 Votes and Proceedings of the House of Commons	White	runs through the session	(a) Official minutes of the previous day's business, excluding Question Time which is an informal proceeding; the time of rising of the House and of the next meeting. (b) Appendices list all the papers presented and laid on the Table on the previous day indicating those ordered to be printed. Also included are appointments to Standing Committees, etc. (*Note:* Together these later form the *Journal* of the House of Commons.)
2 Private Business	White Blue		Business for the day. Notices of future business.
3 Private Bill List	Blue	runs through the session	Cumulating list of private bills showing their progress, published about four times a session, together with all notices concerning private Bills.
4 Public Petitions	White	none: arranged chronologically according to date of entry in the Votes and Proceedings	The text of petitions and the replies of Government Departments to earlier petitions.
5 Public Bill List	White	runs through the session	Cumulating weekly list of public Bills (during session only) with an indication of the stage reached and a list of Standing Committees and Bills allocated to them.

Title	Paper Colour	Pagination	Contents
6 Division Lists	White	runs through the session	A numbered list of the results of each division (with Members' names) together with the text of the motion voted upon.
7 Notices of Motion	White (today) Blue (future)	runs through the session (from session 1979-80 each colour has its own pagination)	(a) Notices of Questions to be asked and of motions to be debated on an 'early day' in the future, the latter having a running number and list of signatories to the motion (on blue paper). A weekly list is published. (b) Order paper for the business on the day of issue including Private business to be taken, Questions for oral answer by Ministers on the day of issue and the text of motions to be debated. List of meetings of Standing Committees and Select Committees giving place and time of meeting, subject of meeting and witnesses and whether a private or public meeting. Questions for written answer that day. Remaining orders and notices of motions for the day of issue (on white paper).
8 Supplement to the Votes and Proceedings of the House of Commons	Blue/White	Various	These papers are linked with Bills going through their Committee stage. They contain the texts of amendments and of new clauses. There is one pagination for the session for Bills taken in the House itself (the whole House). Then there is a new pagination for each new Bill in each of the Standing Committees A, B, C, etc.

THE JOURNAL

The *Journal* of the House of Commons is the authoritative permanent record of
what took place in the House of Commons and also of the papers which have
been laid before the House of Commons. Under the Evidence Act 1845 it is
accepted as evidence in a court of law. The *Journal*, which was first printed in
the eighteenth century, has survived since 1547, except for part of the reign of
Elizabeth I. Unless there is a specific resolution of the House, the *Journal* does
not contain any report of what was said in the House but it does contain the text
of the speeches from the throne (Queen's Speech) which opens and closes each
session. Apart from their printing in the *Journal* and in the Votes and
Proceedings of that day, the Queen's Speeches are only available as leaflets, not
in any numbered series.

Until recently, the text of the *Journal*, which is very much based on the daily
Votes and Proceedings described above, was a recasting of these Votes in
eighteenth century English. In recent years the text of the daily Votes and
Proceedings and the *Journal* have been assimilated.

The *Journal* contains an elaborate index which is in two distinct parts. Part I,
under the heading Accounts and Papers, lists alphabetically by subject all the
papers which have been laid before the House during the session. This includes
the Sessional Papers described below, but also all the papers laid before the
House which it does not order to be printed either because they are already
printed, e.g. some annual reports, or because they are of too limited interest to
be worth printing. In recent years a growing number of important reports
which used to be in the Sessional Papers have been published by organizations
themselves and the House of Commons has not required them to be reprinted
for the House's own Sessional Papers[4]. The result of this is that a series of annual
reports, formerly in the Sessional Papers, ceases to be so, a source of some
irritation to research workers and librarians. Part II of the index covers the
actual proceedings of the House. It is an elaborate index which may at first sight
appear difficult to use but it is designed to reveal the detail of what has taken
place in the House and this it does very well. The *Journal* is one volume for each
session with its own index. The sessional indexes cumulate into one-volume
decennial indexes, the most recent of which covers the sessions 1960-1 to
1969-70. There are 17 volumes of cumulations of indexes going back to 1547.

SESSIONAL PAPERS

The Sessional Papers of the House of Commons consist of Bills, House of
Commons Papers and Command Papers. From 1800 to 1968-69 they were
arranged and indexed in a traditional grouping:

> Public Bills in alphabetical order
> Accounts and Papers
> Reports of Committees
> Reports of Commissioners

In 1969-70 the arrangement and indexing was changed to:

> Public Bills and Minutes of Proceedings in alphabetical order
> Reports, Accounts and Papers arranged alphabetically by subject

From 1979-80 it is proposed to arrange them as Bills, House of Commons Papers and Command Papers, each group separately in number order.

At the end of the last century the number of volumes of Sessional Papers in a single session might run to 130 or so. In recent sessions the number has been 40-50. The volumes in a single session are given roman numbers and the index to the papers, published each session as a House of Commons paper and called the Sessional Index, indicates after the title of the paper, the session in which the paper was published, the number of the paper, the number of the volume and page in the volume where the individual paper begins. A Sessional Index reference to a paper therefore would be:

> Development Fund: Accounts 1972-3; 1973-4 (24) v, 525

meaning that the accounts for the Development Fund for 1972-3 are to be found in the Sessional papers for 1973-4, in Volume V at page 525, where they are House of Commons paper number 24 of that session.

A Sessional Index consists of a numerical list of all Bills starting from 1 each session, a numerical list of all House of Commons papers, starting from 1 each session, and a numerical list of Command papers running through the sessions 1-9999 with a prefix, currently Cmnd. There is in addition a subject index covering all three sets of papers and, finally, a select list of Committee Chairmen and other authors of reports in the index. The subject part of these Sessional Indexes is cumulated every ten years, the most recent being 1959/60 - 1968/69, and then every fifty years, the most recent of these covering 1900-1948/49. Let us now turn to the three groups of Sessional Papers: Bills, House of Commons Papers, and Command Papers.

Bills
After its first reading a Bill is ordered to be printed and given a number, printed in square brackets in the bottom left-hand corner. After the second reading when the principle is discussed it goes into Committee where it may well be amended or new clauses added. When this process is completed it will be reprinted as amended and given a new number in the bottom left-hand corner. There may be further printings of Bills each with a new number but prior to the new arrangement of Sessional Papers starting in 1979-80 the alphabetical arrangement by title of printings of the same Bill and of the Minutes of Proceedings ensures that its changing text is brought together. There are roughly 150 Bills during a session. They are first noticed in the Votes and Proceedings together with their number.

House of Commons Papers
These are papers which have been laid before the House of Commons by its

instruction, e.g. the minutes of evidence or proceedings of a Committee, a report of a Select Committee, the Accounts and/or Reports of an organization, which Parliament requires by Statute, Treasury minutes, etc. After being laid before the House of Commons, the House orders them to be printed. These papers are an important source of information. Over a thousand are laid a session, but only 300–400 of these are ordered to be printed and are to be found in the Sessional Papers. They receive a number printed in the bottom left-hand corner and each of them carries the legend 'ordered to be printed by the House on' such and such a date. The date is the date they are listed in the appendix to the Votes and Proceedings where their number first appears.

Command Papers

These are papers which are laid before the House of Commons by Command of the Queen which really means by the Government. Almost all of them are published and they include reports of Royal Commissions, Government proposals known as 'White Papers', Treaties with foreign countries and international organizations, together with the exchange of other notes, etc. Like other sessional papers they first appear listed in the appendix to the Votes and Proceedings, but their paper number does not become available until they are printed.

The alphabetical index to the Sessional Index brings these three groups of papers together in one subject sequence. They are all available either by subscription or individually from HMSO.

PARLIAMENTARY DEBATES

(a) House of Commons

Finally in this brief account of the papers concerning the House of Commons we come to the Parliamentary Debates (*Hansard*), and the debates of Standing Committees, and the Scottish, Welsh and Northern Ireland Committees. Collections of debates of the House of Commons go back to the Restoration in 1660 and printings of individual speeches even earlier, but it was only in 1909 that the House took over responsibility for reporting its own debates and that the reports became verbatim. Late in 1978 *Hansard* became one of the Departments of the House.

A team of reporters, sitting in the press gallery immediately behind the Speaker's chair, take notes for ten minutes at a time (five minutes in the evening). Their copy is perfected and sent to St Stephen's press in instalments through the day, the latest copy for publication the next morning leaving Westminster at about 11 p.m.

The arrangement of a daily issue of *Hansard* is as follows. Unless the previous day's business has been carried over into the issue, i.e. unless the House sat until after 10.30 p.m. the previous night, the issue will start with the day's Oral Questions and answers. The replies and subsequent supplementary questions may elucidate more politics than information but the dialogue will always be of direct relevance to the political scene. Sometimes they are followed by a statement by a Minister or a special Private Notice Question when the Government passes on information to the House. The second main section of the issue of *Hansard* will contain the report of the main business of the day which may be a debate on a major issue, an important report, or some stage of a Bill. Front-bench spokesmen will lead off with carefully prepared speeches which may contain a lot of information, back-benchers may follow with specialist experience or knowledge, and the front-benchers will probably wind up. If it is a committee stage of a Bill which is being taken in the House of Commons itself then it will appear quite simply as part of the issue and if, as does rarely happen, the second reading of a Bill is taken in a Standing Committee rather than in the House of Commons itself, then this debate will be reported in the House debates rather than the Standing Committee debates. Other debates may follow in the issue and at the end of the day there is a short half-hour adjournment debate on a particular point that a Member will have warned a Minister he is going to raise. All these debates are on a definite motion, the words of which are printed in *Hansard* and if there is a vote on a motion then the Division list is printed. For most people this is the quickest way of finding out who voted which way in a particular debate.

The final section of the issue contains the Written Questions and answers. These are either Oral Questions which there was not enough time to answer, or questions for which Members have requested a written reply. They are very numerous and they contain a great deal of information and very little politics. They have their own sequence of column numbers. Bearing in mind that there are up to 40 000 questions a session and that in addition the House debates about seven or eight hours a day, five days a week for some 36 weeks a year, the magnitude of the information in *Hansard* becomes apparent.

Hansard is published daily and weekly and later in a volume which covers two to three weeks, depending obviously on the length of sittings. There is a weekly index and an index for each volume which can be bought separately from the volume in which it appears. At the end of the session an index covering the session appears as a separate volume. These indexes are strong on names but less so on subjects, especially for debates, as there is virtually no analytical indexing. The numbers in the index refer to columns in *Hansard*, those in ordinary type to the sequence of columns other than the Written Answers at the back, those in italics to these Written Answers. One further piece of information in the first issue of each volume of *Hansard* is a full list of the Government and senior officials at the House of Commons. This is checked each time it is published and is therefore the most up-to-date list published.

(b) Standing Committees, etc.

As we have seen, many Bills go to Standing Committees for detailed examination and the debates of these committees are published each day. This also happens with the debates of the first and second Scottish Standing Committee, the Scottish Grand Committee, the Welsh Grand Committee, the Northern Ireland Committee, and the various Standing Committees on Statutory Instruments.

When a Standing Committee has completed its examination of a Bill then the daily parts of the debates which have been published are collected together and re-published, together with the relevant Bills, in separate brown covers. Much later, maybe two or three years later, the debates of all the committees mentioned above are published in bound form and they are equipped with a name index. This is the only index to Standing Committee debates; it is really no more than a list of speakers, but fairly detailed tables of contents to the daily parts help to identify the subjects covered. Standing Committee debates have been published since 1919.

The Vote Office and the Distribution of Papers

The distribution to Members of the papers is the responsibility of the Deliverer of the Vote, an office which probably dates back to very shortly after the Vote started to be printed in 1680. At first the Vote Office was in the Serjeant at Arms' Department; after 1835 it was in the Speaker's Department; and under the House of Commons Administration Act of 1978 it has recently been transferred to the Library Department.

Members of Parliament are entitled to free copies of the Vote, *Hansard* in all its forms, Bills, Acts, House of Commons Papers, and Command Papers. They may also have copies of papers of the House of Lords. A list of these is circulated to them twice a week, Wednesdays and Saturdays, on a pink form. If Members live within three miles of the Palace of Westminster, then Porters will deliver the chief papers to their homes early each morning. In addition to Members, documents, especially the Vote, are also distributed to Government Departments where the Parliamentary Clerk and his staff need to study them as early in the day as possible.

Although Parliamentary Papers are obviously the most important group of papers distributed by the Vote Office and there are deliveries of new Parliamentary Papers several times a day, increasingly a Minister may decide to deposit in the Vote Office certain non-Parliamentary, mostly HMSO publications, in order to inform Members. The Vote Office requires a minimum number of 100 copies of each of these. As the Vote Office only stores papers of the current session and the preceding one, it has been a Ministerial responsibility since 1961 that where Parliamentary business leads Members' interest back to Parliamentary materials of more than two sessions ago, the Government Department responsible has to send a list of this older material to the Library. Both the list and the material can be consulted in the Library and the Vote Office can obtain copies within two hours to meet the Members' demands.

Apart from the non-Parliamentary papers which Ministers deposit there, the Vote office does not carry a regular supply of Departmental publications, but Members may quickly obtain copies by filling in a green demand form and then stocks are drawn from the Stationery Office itself.

Since 1973 Members have been entitled to the main documentation of the

Table 1.4 Table of Papers and Printed Indexes

Title	Frequency	Indexing	Notes
'Vote'	Sitting days	No	The Votes and Proceedings reproduced in the *Journal* are indexed there; also lists of Bills and of Notices of Motions published weekly
Official Report (*Hansard*) (Whole House)	After sitting days	Weekly. Each volume. Sessional. (separate volume)	*Hansard* is in two sequences so the index to it refers to the sequences 1. In ordinary typeface to all proceedings excluding Written Questions and Answers 2. In italic typeface to Written Questions and Answers
Official Report (*Hansard*) (Standing Committees)	After sitting days of each Committee	No List of speakers only	
Bills House of Commons Papers Command Papers	Irregular	Sessional Index (separate HC Paper) Decennial Index (separate HC Paper) Quindecennial Index (separate HC Paper)	Listed in and therefore indexed in the *Journal* (Part I)
Journal	Sessional	Sessional Index (in the volume) Decennial index (separate volume)	Index, Part I Papers, Part II Proceedings

All this material except the 'Vote' is listed in the HMSO Daily List and Monthly and Annual Catalogue of Government Publications.

European Communities such as the Official Journal and its Annex, the Working Documents of the European Parliament, and also the Draft Regulations which are examined by the relevant Select Committee in both Houses (see p. 71) together with the Government Memorandum on each one. About a hundred copies of each are taken. This had led to great storage problems and it is fortunate that the House of Commons took over the Norman Shaw (North) building at about this time and that it has been possible to centre the main collection of these European documents outside the Palace of Westminster. Members of Parliament are informed of these European papers through a weekly yellow demand form which is distributed with the Vote on Thursdays.

The scale of the work of the Vote Office is immense. Estimates suggest that in 1946 some 850 000 documents were handled. This had grown to some 3 200 000 by 1979 and the latest estimates are even higher. But it is not the scale of the operation which is crucial. Members are very sensitive about being informed on matters by the Government and the work of the Vote Office is centred on this vital area. A Member who considers that he and other Members have not been supplied with the documents for the business at hand can appeal to the Speaker or his Deputy to adjourn the debate. When such an appeal is successful it is annoying and indeed humiliating for the Government of the day.

In recent years a tendency has arisen for certain organizations that are formally required to lay their report and accounts before Parliament to do so only with a 'dummy' paper. They then publish the paper themselves, rather than the Stationery Office, and the result is that it receives no House of Commons number, fails to get into the bound set of House of Commons Papers, into the Sessional index and its Cumulations, and also into the Vote Office for Members. A list of reports in this group is to be found in Appendix 4.

The Vote Office is open from 7 a.m. to the rising of the House five days a week, and because of its work the Library does not issue copies of official papers to Members, and is therefore able to treat official publications as non-loanable reference material. This ensures that should the 'Chair', i.e. the Speaker or his Deputy, send to the Library for an official document because of an important point raised in debate, then the reference copy is immediately available.

The Library

There are various approaches to describing a living institution. One option is the historical, which is not appropriate here because this is meant to be an outline of the Library and its work in the late 1970s. A second is the administrative analysis which tends to dissect an organization, a useful management tool. A third option, the one followed here, is to try and describe it as an organism, showing the interdependence of the need (the Member of Parliament), the means of meeting it (the staff and the material and its organization), and the result (the output).

BACKGROUND

At the time of writing, the House of Commons Library is 160 years old and in view of the ancient and traditional nature of the working of the House itself, a brief historical introduction is essential.

The earliest properly designated and organized **Parliamentary Library in**

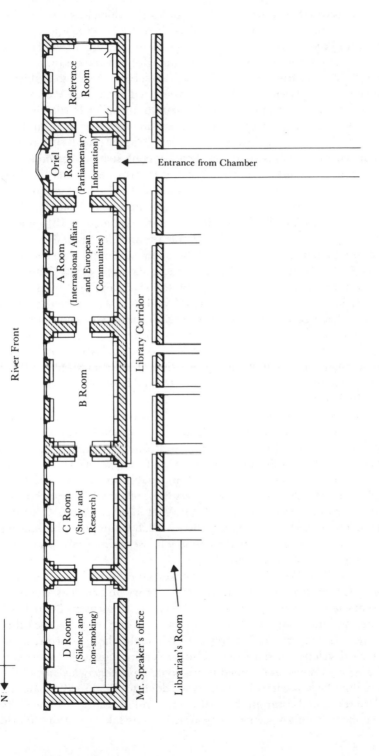

Layout of rooms in the Commons Library

these islands was that of the Irish House of Lords, which was active in the 1790s pressing for more accommodation. The Irish Parliament was abolished in 1800. In the same year Charles Abbot, a great collector and organizer of records and books, became Chief Secretary in Ireland. He personally saw to it that the Library of the old Irish House of Lords was safely removed to Dublin Castle. Following this experience in 1802 he was elected Speaker at Westminster and returned to take the documentary problems of the older Parliament in hand. The Irish Parliament had been housed in the first modern European Parliament House which Arthur Young called 'appartments spacious, elegant and convenient, much beyond that heap of confusion at Westminster'.[4] This confusion at Westminster extended to the records and a small collection of books, which were in the immediate custody of the Clerk of the Journals, who, about 1800, collected them together in his residence in Abingdon Street.

The first Librarian, Benjamin Spiller, was appointed in 1818 and he was given a room about 17 ft square, just beside the ancient Westminster Hall. This was soon too small and by 1826 Sir John Soane was putting up a new, elegant Library 55 × 23 ft, detailed in the fashionable and appropriate Gothic style. In 1832 the Library was again found to be too small and two committee rooms over the Library were added to it so that by 1833 it was more than ten times the area of Spiller's Library of 1818. It was this Library with most of its contents which was burnt when the Palace of Westminster went up in flames in 1834. Barry's plans for the new Palace of Westminster envisaged a main floor with both chambers on it and along the fine river front a succession of handsome rooms which included the suite of rooms of the House of Lords Library which physically balances the Commons Library.

During the period until 1862 the Library was carefully watched over and examined by a regularly appointed Committee, sometimes sprinkled with such familiar names as Gladstone, Disraeli, Lord John Russell, etc. The new rooms were occupied about 1852 and during the first forty-five years a great number of catalogues and indexes were compiled and published. From 1862 to 1922, a period when Members were mostly very well off, the Library seems to have rested on its oars, remaining a 'Library of Historical and Constitutional Information' as had been required by an 1828 Committee, but adding in a desultory way, the dimension of a country house/club library which matched the ethos of most of the Members.

After the First World War, the Speaker established in 1922 an informal advisory Committee to help him run the Library on behalf of Members, and two years later the historian, H A L Fisher, its Chairman, invited a fellow Member and historian, Sir Charles Oman, to write a report on the Library. It was a trenchant report, questioning, as well it might, the sense of direction of the Library's development since the mid-nineteenth century. A decade later, the zeal of Ivor Jennings, as revealed in his book *Parliamentary Reform* published in 1934 calling for a modern Library, was added to the muted debate. In 1937 Mr Kitto became Librarian; he had been Assistant Librarian since 1908 and the likelihood of reform seemed no nearer. It was to take the Second World War to crack the traditional mould of the Library. About two-thirds of the books were removed for the duration of the War and this may have helped to clear minds on the subject.

In December 1944 Kitto handed a memorandum on the Library to the Speaker who passed it on to a Select Committee appointed in April 1945 just three months before the Labour Party's election victory. Kitto, with the sweeping insight of one on the verge of retirement after some 36 years on the staff, wrote not without a touch of frustration:

> No thorough effort to reorganise the Library in the House of Commons has been made since it was moved into the rooms, which it still occupies, shortly after the completion of the present Palace in the middle of the last century. It is submitted that this is a state of affairs which cannot any longer endure if Members, particularly new Members entering Parliament for the first time, are to be provided with a modern up-to-date library.[5]

Among those Members who read this evidence and nodded their assent to this direct proposition were the author Harold Nicolson, the Cambridge historian Kenneth Pickthorn, and the Chairman of the Speaker's Library Advisory Committee, George Benson. Fifteen years later, as Sir George Benson, and still Chairman of the Committee on the Library, he told the Estimates Committee: 'As a back-bench Member in 1930, I was appalled to find the House of Commons served by a Library which had hardly progressed since 1850... Latin and French classics still occupied front-room space in the exact positions where they had been originally placed in 1852'.[6] It was this 1945 Committee which was to propose letting in the twentieth century, and on its recommendations the Library's post-war development has been based.

MEMBERS

Members of Parliament are buffeted by information. But it is not just that there is a great deal of it; nearly everyone who sets out to inform them has some case to make. Consider briefly their sources of information as a background to the Library's role.

Firstly, there is the Member's constituency – his mail, his 'surgery' in which he regularly meets individual constituents, local government dignatories, and the local press. Over the week-end or during recesses he will soak up a thousand facts, a hundred impressions, all of them derived from the particular problems of his particular constituency. The information is valuable and important, but not impartial.

Second, there is the civil service. The Member returns from his constituency prompted to interrogate the Executive about problems. He will glean a great deal of information through Parliamentary Questioning and by interrogating departmental witnesses before Select Committees, but even so the civil servant has a first loyalty to his current minister, and that will influence the information that he provides.[7]

Third, there are the particular lobbies who will, by definition, be arranging the information they send him in order to put across their point of view.

Fourth, there is his own political party, busy helping those on the front benches or researching long-term policies. They do, of course, help their own Members, deftly adding political gloss to the facts and keeping everyone up to the party line.

Fifth, there are the two sides of industry who come to present a case either because of constituency problems or because of a Member's known interest or expertise.

Finally, there are the other leads in to a Member – the Embassy reception, membership of a group with particular interests, a neighbour at a dinner party, a word with a colleague in a corridor.

All these sources of information are essentially political in their motivation and this suits the Member, because he is a politician trying to achieve certain priorities for the development of our society, based on his political principles. But for many Members, there is a point at which, in terms of information, the shouting has to stop; he must have quietness and impartiality, he needs to place questions with qualified staff who respond to him as an individual, not really as a political or indeed public figure and whose advice, if asked for, is non-political. It is at this point that he can and often does turn to the House of Commons Library. That is its unique role: to be a source of confidential information for Members of Parliament from increasingly specialist staff who have no axe to grind but who know the way in which the House of Commons works. No other source of information can serve him in quite the same way as the Library of the House.

Barry placed the Library of the House of Commons so that it overlooked the river and is just fifty paces from the Chamber. It lies between the Smoking Room and the Tea Room and over the Strangers' Bar – an ideal position midst these other essential services for Members. The situation of the Library, on the private side of the Palace of Westminster opening off the busiest corridors in the building is better than any parliamentary library I know. It can be opened at any time for a Member and is staffed from 9 a.m. until the rising of the House and on Saturday mornings – an average of over 70 hours a week. It is comfortable to write in, to read in, to research in, to rest in; above all, except during very restricted hours, it is private to Members who are beyond the reach of the outside world. It is difficult to estimate the number of Members who use the Library. Some use it several times a day, a few very seldom. Barker and Rush, in their analysis of Library use in 1967, interviewed 111 Members and suggest that 72 per cent of Members used the Library at least once a day, 3.7 per cent less than once a week, and the rest somewhere between the two. Of those who used the Library, a higher number came for information than for any other service, 75 per cent to ask for information, 64 per cent to borrow material, and 62 per cent to read newspapers, journals, etc. The Library is also used by Members for writing speeches and attending to correspondence and other work.

Since 1967 a somewhat different pattern has emerged as far more Members have their own rooms and a growing number of Members have their own research assistants. The result of these factors is to reduce the use of the Library accommodation during hours when the House is not sitting. However, once the outside world has closed down, the telephones have stopped, and the majority of staff have gone home, then the Members return to their former routine and the Library once again becomes an essential haunt for many of them.

It seems to me that there are several advantages for a Member in using the House of Commons Library. First, the Library is at his elbow, virtually always open, staffed and organized to work to the level required and to very tight deadlines. Second, it provides a personal and confidential service so that Members need not reveal their hand either to civil servants or to their parties. Before breaking into the political world on a specific subject, a Member can prepare himself in privacy but with experienced assistance. Third, the staff, who work daily with members, can sometimes take short-cuts which may be very helpful to them. Fourth, the Member can stipulate exactly why and in what form he wants information.

A Member uses the Library for a variety of reasons, apart from simply as a place to read or write. He will use its facilities to prepare a speech in the House, to secure background for a speech in Standing Committee or for his questioning in a Select Committee, or to get ready to represent his party on a broadcast. All these activities are in a public arena. He may have a handful of constituency letters he would like help in considering, or he may need background information before lunching with a foreign celebrity or travelling in a delegation abroad. These would be more private activities. He may have just become a member of a party group on defence, or on, say, Anglo–Yugoslav relations, or on a certain aspect of transport and wish 'to start from scratch' on these subjects. These are just a few of the reasons that might explain why a Member would come to the Library.

ORGANIZATION AND STAFF

In as much as there are any terms of reference for the Library, they are enshrined in the views of the already mentioned Select Committee on Library (House of Commons) whose first report in November 1945 set down:

> Your Committee think that the essential purpose of the House of Commons Library is to supply Members with information rapidly on any of the multifarious matters which come before the House or to which their attentions are drawn by their parliamentary duties.[8]

At the end of the Second World War this was modern library thinking, although today we can see it as prompted by new political and social thinking partly created by the War. It was, however, a fundamental commitment in the Library's development. The second important innovation, also at this time, was to decide to put the research services in the Library, rather than to follow the not uncommon but expensive and inefficient method of separating them from it. Three later stages in Library development must be briefly mentioned.

First, in the second Report from the Estimates Committee 1960-1, it was recommended that newcomers to the Library Clerk grade should no longer be linked to the Civil Service museum keeper grade but to the lower Civil Service executive grade.[9] This was rejected by Mr Speaker's Advisory Committee.[10] Had it been accepted, it would have been impossible to sustain research services for long. Second, in 1966, following Treasury O and M inspection, the organization of the Library as outlined below was agreed and it looks likely to form the pattern for many years to come. Third, in 1967, the Library became a separate Department of the House and the post of Deputy Librarian was created, both events recognizing its growing size and importance in the provision of services to Members.

The Librarian and the Deputy Librarian of the House of Commons are appointed by the Speaker and subsequently the Librarian appoints all other members of his staff, since 1979 under powers delegated to him by the House of Commons Commission. He has worked, since 1966, directly to a Select Committee of the House, namely the Library Sub-Committee of the House of Commons (Services) Committee. The Librarian is also a member of the Board of Management of the House of Commons which is made up of the heads of the House of Commons Departments. It is this body which is responsible for carrying out the broad policy on House of Commons matters laid down by the Commissioners, all of whom are Members with Mr Speaker as Chairman. The Deputy Librarian is, with fellow deputies and other senior colleagues, one from each Department, a member of the Administration Committee of the Board of Management. This body considers all interdepartmental staff matters, makes recommendations to the Accounting Officer concerning new staff, grading etc., and acts as the management side in many trade union matters. He also acts as departmental Establishment Officer and Security Officer.

Below these two posts, the Library breaks into two Divisions. The first of these is the Research Division, the second the Parliamentary Division (more clearly designated for the reader as the Library Division), which centres its activities on non-research services. Each of these Divisions comes under an Assistant Librarian. The next and really the smallest unit of organization – though they vary greatly in size and seniority of staff – is the Section and many of these come under a Deputy Assistant Librarian. Certain Sections in the Library or Parliamentary division are headed at a lower grade.

All House of Commons staff are linked to a grade in the Civil Service and their terms and conditions of service are similar, making allowance for the irregular demands of the working of the House of Commons. This means that the senior grade of staff, following the Librarian (Under Secretary) and Deputy Librarian (Assistant Secretary), is linked to the Museum (Curator) grade as follows: Assistant Librarians (Grade A), Deputy Assistant Librarians (Grade B), Senior Library Clerks (Grades C and D) and Assistant Library Clerks (Grades E and F). This senior grade of staff, who are to be found in both Divisions, are recruited through open competition run by the Civil Service Commission, though there are occasional internal promotions. There are two

Assistant Librarians, seven Deputy Assistant Librarians and 17 Library Clerks. The middle grade of staff who, if not promoted from within, are recruited directly through the House of Commons Establishment Office through open competition, are a mixture of professional librarians and non-professional staff. Many of the professional librarians are recruited direct, most of the non-professional middle-grade staff are promotees. Naturally, non-professional staff are encouraged to secure professional qualifications, which speeds their promotion. There are 28 staff in these grades, which span the Civil Service executive officer grade to the senior executive officer grade (or their Librarian grade equivalent). Of these 28, 16 are professionally qualified.

The supporting staff includes 13 clerical grade staff, 17 secretarial staff and ten paperkeeper grade staff. Five part-time cleaners spend several hours of every day cleaning the collections of Library materials. The cost of running the Library Department, including the Vote Office, is to be found in Civil Estimates (Class XIII.A) and the figures for 1979–80 were £719 000 for staff and £116 000 for materials and binding and other services called 'general expenses'. So much for the broad organization and the main grades of staff. We can now turn to the more detailed organization chart (see Fig. 1.1).

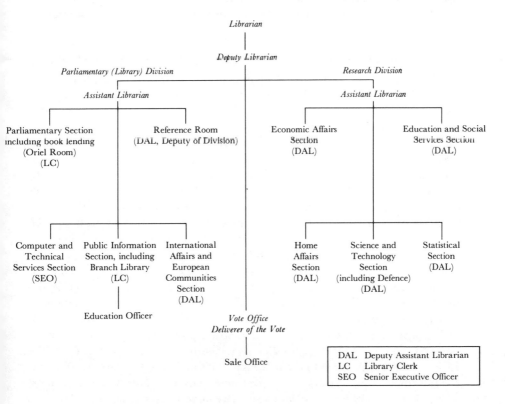

Fig. 1.1   Library Department House of Commons, organization chart

Research Division

The Research Division under an Assistant Librarian consists of five Sections, each under a Deputy Assistant Librarian. The Deputy Assistant Librarian is responsible for the output of his Section and is helped by two or three Library Clerks. Each Section also has a professional librarian, who often undertakes some of the quicker, less specialized enquiries and offers the bibliographical support the research staff need. Finally there is the clerical and the secretarial staff, on whom so much depends, and the number of these varies from Section to Section, according to the size of their own collections of material and the breadth of their subject coverage.

All Library Clerk staff are recruited on the basis of their academic achievement, a resilient temperament, their clarity, fluency and accuracy of expression, and their willingness to accept a rather anonymous role. It is, after all, the Member who is going to personalize the information. Increasingly, at this level, and especially for the Research Division, the Library is looking for specialist staff such as statisticians, economists and, more recently, one with legal qualifications. There are normally a number of foreign linguists among the staff too, although all of them do not have much scope for their professional skills. Library qualifications are always an advantage but the criteria outlined above must also be met. All staff are liable for transfer from one Division to another.

If one considers Parliamentary affairs it is obvious that Members' interests range very widely. Because of the very long hours that the Library is open there is a considerable chance that a particular specialist may not be on duty when a Member wishes to consult him. Staff must, therefore, be ready to turn their hand quickly to subjects other than their own. In this respect, the work resembles serious journalism though we would like to think it is more accurate and that for a very specific reason. Information given to a Member may immediately become public property. He may quote it within five minutes in the Chamber, he may use it for a TV interview that night. However he uses it, he would look very foolish and his arguments collapse, if a key fact had been left out, or staff had put a decimal point too far to the left, or the right!

In addition to breadth, flexibility and accuracy of approach, staff must be prepared to take personal responsibility for the work they prepare. There are too many questions and too few staff to guarantee that more than a small number of answers are checked by others before they go to a Member. This is in strong contrast to most large organizations, such as the Civil Service or the nationalized industries, where information sent to Parliament will have been vetted several times.

The way in which staff organize their work, provided they meet Members' demands in a way that does not disturb the equilibrium and reputation of the Library, is left very much to them. This is as it should be, as in no two subjects is the information pattern the same. Drawing help from outside organizations, whether in the public or private sector, is sometimes a delicate and always rather a personal matter. There are, however, certain practical constraints.

Field-work to obtain information is not undertaken and it is normally impractical for staff to undertake much work away from the Palace of Westminster. It is for this reason, and the unusual hours the Library works, that it takes and processes a great deal of material especially in the broad area of public policy and the social services.

While subject enquiries form the bulk of the work of the Research Division, two forms of information may permeate all subjects on which replies are given, namely, statistics and law. While statistics are always prepared by statisticians, all staff are expected to handle the legal aspects of their subjects, although a legally qualified member of staff can be consulted.

The Research Division staff are scattered through the building and some are now outside it. In order to maintain that close contact with Members which is such an essential feature of work at the House of Commons and which differentiates it from many parliamentary libraries, one room in the main Library suite is set aside for the Research Division. Here, most Sections have a senior member of staff available for Members to discuss with and hand in enquiries to and where they may obtain immediate oral information.

Parliamentary (Library) Division
The Parliamentary or Library Division is under an Assistant Librarian, with the support of a deputy who is graded Deputy Assistant Librarian and who runs the Reference Room which is mostly manned at the middle grade.

Next door to the Reference Room is the Oriel Room, the centre of Parliamentary information for Members. This is the responsibility of a Senior Library Clerk and other staff are at the senior, middle and clerical grades. The next room, A room, holds the International Affairs Section which is organized like a Research Division Section under a Deputy Assistant Librarian with two Library Clerks, a professional librarian and supporting staff. The Section covers foreign affairs, including the work of intergovernmental organizations, and gives comparative information in the area of education and the social services. For other subjects, the Research Division provides information on a world-wide basis. Within the International Affairs Section is the European Communities desk, created on 1 January 1973 when Britain joined the EEC and staff here handle the considerable documentation from the community institutions, especially the European Parliament.

All the staff of the Parliamentary or Library Division mentioned so far work in the main suite of Library rooms, continuously in contact with members and dealing with a great number of oral enquiries every day. But there are two sections of this Division which are situated away from the Library proper. The first of these is the Public Information Section which was only introduced in 1978 and which is situated in the Norman Shaw (North) building, previously Scotland Yard. This building provides a great deal of accommodation for Members and their personal staff and also includes a Branch Library. This is the centre for answering a growing number of enquiries from members of the public, government departments, business firms, the media etc. Until a few years ago, these enquiries by phone and letter came directly into the Oriel Room. They were naturally mostly for Parliamentary information, where they clashed with the direct service to Members which was undertaken in the same room. Today this busy area has been moved out of the Palace of Westminster. (More detail of the work of this Section is given on p. 89.)

The second Section in the Parliamentary Division not working directly with Members is the Computer and Technical Services Section. It was formed in April 1980 because of the reorganization required in connection with the Library's computer-based indexing plans. This is an all-professional Section with supporting staff which consists firstly of the old established Cataloguing Unit the duties of which are rather broader than its name suggests. It is here that material is ordered and catalogued and it is also responsible for the assembly of most of the Library binding of pamphlets, Stationery Office publications etc. Currently it houses the Library's BLAISE Terminal. Secondly, there is the new Indexing Unit currently being built up and trained to undertake the input for the computer-based indexing system (see p. 78) including the maintenance of the Library's Thesaurus prepared for this purpose. The Section, which is housed in the Norman Shaw (South) building is really a servicing Section for the Library as a whole.

Before concluding this survey of the various Sections of the Library, I should add that although it is a unified Library, in addition to the main Library holdings, Research Division Sections have their own small collections and three Sections in the Library have separate sub-libraries, two of them very substantial. The first of these is the Statistics Section which since its establishment in 1946 has always held its collection together and which now has a really substantial library. The second is the International Affairs Section which has an even greater collection; its stock dates back in some cases to 1919 and it holds all the United Nations material and that of a great number of other intergovernmental agencies and organizations which have sprung up since the War, as well as US Congressional documentation and official publications of other countries. The third is the Library of the Scientific Section which dates from 1966. Although it is a small collection, it is designed to respond to Members' needs to keep abreast of the whole range of policy in scientific, technical, and defence matters.

The Library grew from a staff of six in 1946 to over a hundred in 1980. It is never easy when an organization grows to meet varying needs, and without a blueprint being prepared at the beginning, to have as symmetrical an organization as a draughtsman might like. Broadly speaking, the emphasis in the Research Division is on written response and written anticipatory work together with oral help in subject areas. All other activities of the Library, including the work of the Computer and Technical Services Section, are situated in the Parliamentary or Library Division. In this Division the emphasis is on non-specialist quick oral information, sometimes with written responses, and all the operations undertaken by professional staff for the Library as a whole.

MATERIALS AND SERVICES

The Library of the House of Commons is not really very large. An estimate of 150 000 volumes would not be too wide of the mark. To this, however, would have to be added a great deal of official material both domestic and foreign.

The first 'Catalogue of Books in the Library at the House of Commons' was published as House of Commons Paper 80 of Session 1829-30. The original interleaved copy put in the 'Upper Library' survives with an introduction by John Rickman. This copy includes some manuscript amendments up to and including 1834, but the main catalogue in use then was destroyed in the fire. Works on history, law, Parliamentary records and the reports of the Record Commission so active at that time, predominate. A rough list of books which were destroyed in the 1834 fire (mostly in the Upper Library) and of those which survived (mostly in the Lower Library), published in a report in 1835, suggests about two-thirds of the stock was destroyed and subsequently £3000 was requested to replenish the Library.

Two important collections reached the Library subsequent to the fire. The first was of eighteenth century printed Parliamentary papers covering 1731-1800 which had been bound up under instructions from Speaker Abbot at the beginning of the nineteenth century and which is therefore known as the 'Abbot Collection'. The second was of some 1,110 pamphlets covering 1559-1740, including many official papers, and which was kept in the Gallery in the Speaker's House and thus escaped the fire. In 1805 the pamphlets had been bound up into 91 volumes, again by Speaker Abbot's instructions, and arrived in the Library in 1837. In 1856 and again in 1889 a Catalogue of them was printed.

For the century after the fire, the stock of the Library was built up on sound nineteenth century humanist principles. All the standard historical material is to be found, like the Public Records, the Historical Manuscript Commission publications which for much of the time were Command papers and the eighteenth and nineteenth century county and local histories. All are important because Members are nearly always interested in the history of their constituency and many of these publications impinge not only on the history of politics but also of Parliament. Parallel with these volumes are good collections of topography and literature and standard works on philosophy and religion.

During the early twentieth century it seems that book purchasing was reduced, perhaps because space was a problem, so that by the end of the Second World War much of the stock was out of touch with Members' needs. Throughout this period (from 1834 onwards), catalogues were regularly printed, especially once the Library had been installed in the new Barry building in 1852. In the 1860s, subject indexes were started and both author and subject catalogues continued to be printed regularly until the last full catalogue came out in 1910. Supplements then completed the story until the end of the Second World War (see pp. 51-2).

Among this earlier material there are a certain number of very beautiful and valuable works, no incunabula, but the majority of books would be familiar on the shelves of a really good old-established club library. It is not possible to go into detail about this stock in a work concerned with the 1980s, but it can be said that the nineteenth century Library collection is well founded.

Today the selection of material is widely based among Library staff and the subject specialists should not have any great difficulty getting material which they need or believe Members will need. The Members themselves are free to make suggestions and do so, but as with most libraries a great number of books and pamphlets choose themselves. It might be best to walk through the Library and look at the material for ourselves (see p. 21).

If we start in the Reference Room, which is crowded and busy, we find it is the centre of atlases and maps, of a great collection of UK town guides, and of hundreds of annual reports from institutions (few from companies). The collection of newspapers is an extensive one, including quite a number from the major European countries and from the Commonwealth. National and most regional dailies are displayed together with a representative collection of the foreign press. The Library keeps files of *The Times* and *The Guardian* permanently (now on microfilm) and of other papers, up to four years. On days when the House sits, the Serjeant at Arms' Department supplies Members' public rooms with more local papers so that while they attend at Westminster they can keep abreast of local developments.

A second group of material is the periodicals. Between 1500 and 2000 titles are taken in the Reference Room, about one-quarter of which are kept permanently. Between 150 and 200 of these titles are of general interest, some of them leisure reading. This is not surprising in view of the very long hours that Members are kept at Westminster. By far the majority, however, are taken for the relevance of their subject content to Members' work. It is difficult to set down what the last sentence covers but some guidelines on what is needed suggest themselves.

The House of Commons is concerned with helping to identify problems, legislating on them, examining the administration of this legislation together with the expenditure of public funds, and also contributing to the national debate on foreign relations. If that is their work, life for Members is a matter of politics, i.e. they are elected so that a government can be formed to achieve certain priorities. Because of these two aspects, the Library needs to take material of both fact and opinion. The facts in the periodicals must be as authoritative as possible. First, then, there are the government and other official periodicals which, unless they are very specialized, are needed by Members both for their facts and the gloss that the government of the day is putting on them. Second, there are journals which are offering alternative sets of facts to those of the government (the *NIESR Review*) or offering facts in an area where the government does not do so to any great extent (*New Community*). The opinion on government policy or its administration in journals may be from a general point of view (*Country Life* on our heritage) or a more specialist viewpoint (*Library Association Record* on library matters). There are also the journals on politics and on Parliament, the law journals, and journals of official information from abroad, together with those from intergovernmental organizations.

Members of Parliament are living in a practical world so that the number of heavyweight academic journals is small. In economics, for instance, it is applied economic information they need, like banking reviews, rather than journals of economic theory, and the same would apply in areas such as science and technology, where it is the policy and results of science which they need to understand rather than the method.

A third group of material in the Reference Room is provided by central government, the collections of papers which they distribute to organizations and individuals, offering instruction, advice or just information. Members are often drawn into the relationship between government and the individual and they need to know how they are linked. This material covers press notices, departmental circulars, leaflets, and the great library of welfare state information which at times we all need.

The Reference Room holds considerable collections of press-cuttings on UK matters. The *Times* newspaper each day sends some scores of cuttings of the previous day's paper which are kept in files under the same headings as at the *Times* newspaper itself. In addition, Library staff themselves make extensive selective cuttings of comment from the dozen leading daily newspapers and weekly journals. A further filed service available is that of Extel Cards which conveniently draw together a great deal of up-to-date company information.

Finally, there is the ordinary reference stock which measures up to a medium-size collection, the contents of which, be it dictionaries, encyclopaedias, directories or reference books would be familiar to all using or working in reference libraries. The index specially linked to the material in this room is the Home (UK) Affairs Index.

If we pass into the Oriel Room, next to the Reference Room, we will find it equally crowded and busy. The materials here are mostly connected with Parliament. There are debates in both Houses, including Standing Committee Debates of the House of Commons, which tell us what was said in Parliament, and the Commons Vote Bundle and the Lords Minutes, together with the *Journal* of each House which tell us what was done. The Statutes Revised and the Public Government Acts, a set especially amended with the Annual Annotations to Acts, tell us about current Statute Law; Local and Personal Acts are also kept, and Statutory Instruments to tell us about delegated legislation. A set of Sessional Papers of both Houses together with the papers actually laid before the House of Commons keep us up-to-date with information presented to the House. There are papers specially placed in the Library by Ministers for Members to consult, and in this room one asks for Government Departmental publications and Northern Ireland papers. The indexes, especially linked to the material in this room, are the Parliamentary Index, the Bill Index, the Parliamentary Questions Index, and the Chairman's Index.

'A' Room (next to the Oriel Room) where we move next is the documentation centre for International Affairs and for the European Communities. The Library is in practice, if not in name, a deposit library for the United Nations. Some of their material, notably Security Council papers, is actually flown over from New York and received very quickly via the Foreign Office. All the agencies of the UN, from the ILO which worked under the League of Nations to UNESCO, FAO, WHO, IAEA, etc. send their publications. The European organizations like OECD are fully covered and also others where Members have a form of direct membership such as the Council of Europe and the Western European Union. The Library receives all material from the US Congress and some publications from the US government agencies and other foreign states.

At a lower level than the official documents themselves, most of these organizations have a highly developed press relations side and it is certainly essential to take their press office material.

Within the International Affairs Section is the European Communities Desk. Here are to be found those publications of the European Commission, Council, Court and Parliament normally available and, in addition, the detailed internal papers of the European Parliament and all the drafts of European Secondary legislation. The indexes especially linked to the material in this room are the International Affairs Index, the European Communities Index and the European Secondary Legislation Index. A press-cuttings service is prepared as a back-up to the working of the International Affairs Section.

The International Affairs and the European Communities material we see in this room is only a small fraction of the International Affairs Section's large sub-library mentioned later.

The rest of 'A' Room is devoted to law, international law and monographs connected with the work of the International Affairs Section.

The next room, 'B' Room, (without staff) contains a large collection of books on miscellaneous subjects (excluding literature, history, travel and biography) and an extensive collection of modern pamphlets. Pamphlet material is of great importance for at least two reasons. First, it is very much more up-to-date when first published than are books. Second, it is the way in which small groups, even individuals, can bring pressure to bear on Members. Often it is the only way in which it is possible to afford to publish information at all. For these reasons the buying of pamphlets is an important duty of the Library.

When we reach the next room, 'C' Room, we are again in the presence of Library staff, this time an outpost of Research Division Subject Sections, and clearly they need their immediate sources. The majority of the room is, however, devoted to history and biography.

The final room, 'D' Room, is for Members only, a silence and no smoking room, in which the main collections are literature, travel, bibliography and a full run of the House of Commons *Journal*. In the Library Corridor outside the Library suite is the great run of Parliamentary Papers from the eighteenth century onwards, a run of *Hansard* from 1800 onwards and an important collection of Government Departmental publications.

The House of Commons Library's collection of books on Parliament is of course substantial, but not particularly distinguished. Pre-1800 debates are strong and reference has already been made to the collections of Parliamentary papers and pamphlets which came to the Library after the fire. But at no time has there been a systematic attempt to collect the early printed papers, or printed sermons to the House of Commons for instance, and other contemporary sources. The focus of the House of Commons Library is more on the present and future. Modern studies are bought, whether on the history of Parliament or its present working, but there is no policy of comprehensively buying older material.

It has already been mentioned that there are three distinct sub-libraries, run by the International Affairs, the Scientific, and the Statistics Sections.

The first of these is large. It includes papers of the International Labour Organization from 1919, including records, periodicals and other publications. There are also the US Senate Documents, Reports and Committee Hearings and similar papers of the House of Representatives, going back about thirty years. The Congressional Record takes their debates back to the Second World War and there are collections of Acts, Treaties etc. Commonwealth Parliamentary papers make up a very extensive collection though their use declines as the demand for the European Communities documents increases. There are great UN collections, from their first meeting only a few yards away in the Central Hall, Westminster, to date, together with the great range of publications of the UN's specialist agencies. This large, separate sub-library, mostly in the Palace itself, is arranged by a simple system of prefixed letters and the organization's own serial number where this is possible, the material being selectively indexed on the International Affairs Index or the European Communities Index.

The Scientific Section sub-library is very different. In 1966 there were, of course, books on science and technology and the Section adapted the main Library system for its own quite extensive collection of monographs. This arrangement was not specific enough, however, for articles, pamphlets etc. These are arranged by UDC with an alphabetical subject strip index and the press-cuttings collection of the Section is arranged by these same headings. Recently the sub-library has been moved to the Norman Shaw (South) building.

To reach the third sub-library – that of the Statistics Section – we leave the Palace of Westminster for the Norman Shaw (North) building, known to generations as the police headquarters of Scotland Yard. During the early 1970s it was taken over for the House of Commons and carefully converted for modern use. Two sections of the Library have moved there and the first of these was the Statistics Section.

There are four full-time graduate staff engaged in statistical research work over a very wide range of national and international material. The Section has existed since 1946, it was the only specialist Section for many years and it possesses substantial holdings. Official papers predominate, from the UK or foreign governments, the proliferating intergovernmental organizations and other recognized sources. The UK historic collections are quite strong: the first official census was in 1801, organized by the same John Rickman who signed the House of Commons Library Catalogue of 1830. Today among other important sources are the replies to Parliamentary Questions, so the Section keeps a special index to these – if they contain figures in the answer.

Each of these three sub-libraries is maintained by a professional librarian and the Section decides its own broad policy on expenditure, holdings, binding etc. Each has its own indexing system but it is clear that when the Library's main indexing system is transferred to a computer and a general thesaurus is used, the present methods will have to be re-examined.

The second collection in the Norman Shaw (North) building is that of the Branch Library opened in 1975. This is largely a duplication of some of the current material in the Reference and Oriel Rooms and it is especially strong in current Parliamentary material as the new Public Information Office, which mostly answers questions on Parliament, was grafted on to it in 1978. It is here that the House of Commons *Weekly Information Bulletin* is prepared.

The Branch Library is where microfilm is being introduced on quite a large scale. *The Times, Sunday Times* and the three supplements are taken together with *The Economist* and *Hansard,* and through an arrangement with the House of Lords Library, which microfilms the House of Commons Library's UK press cuttings, a copy of this microfiche is made available. A beginning, therefore, is being made to introduce Members' Secretaries and Research Assistants to microform and an extensive programme is planned for the future.

This is a summary account of the Library's materials. We have not walked through the cellars of the Palace with sets of the six-inch Ordnance Survey maps, complete runs of journals like the *Illustrated London News, Punch, Notes and Queries,* or *The Listener.* We have not crossed the river to look at reserve stock kept under Waterloo Station in areas where vodka was bottled until recent years, nor climbed the Victoria Tower to a floor loaned to the Library which holds among other items a complete set of the *London Gazette* from 1666, and the original special papers deposited by Ministers since 1836.

Every working day and many times a day a great quantity of material arrives addressed to the House of Commons Library. Much of this is free, as it comes from an official source or through the generosity of publishers, not normally book publishers, but the Library does spend considerable sums (in 1979–80 about £70 000), on the routine buying of printed and microform material. But before turning to the question of how this is being indexed and catalogued, reference must be made to the way in which some £14 500 is spent on special services.

Mention has already been made of *The Times* daily cuttings service and the Extel card service. More long-standing than either of those is the Book Loans Service which is conducted from the Oriel Room. About 5 000 items a year are borrowed, about two-thirds being from the Library's own stock, the rest from outside sources. A large subscription to the Harrod's lending library for current books and to the London Library and others for older or more specialist material, together with generous co-operation from outside libraries, public, academic and government departments, helps Library staff to supply a sharp service. As with other aspects of the Library's work, Members expect a response, if the material must be borrowed from outside, in hours rather than days. The recent facility to use the National Lending Library direct via a BLAISE terminal is a significant advance.

Two further services should be mentioned. First, there is a new Videotape service by which the BBC and ITA supply regularly the videotapes of a number of programmes of interest to Members. These are kept for a fortnight and are made available on demand. There is also the possibility that Members can request particular programmes. This service was introduced following a recommendation of the Services Committee. It was originally started to keep Welsh and Scottish Members in touch with the opinion of their home countries during debates on the devolution question, and has proved of considerable interest, especially on regional matters.

Second, following a decision by the Services Committee on 6 December 1977, an experimental scheme for access on behalf of Members to the Treasury Model of the UK was started. The macro-economic model is a simplified representation of the way in which the economic system works based on the way in which it is thought to have worked in the past. Members discuss their requirements with suitably qualified Library staff who then formulate the enquiry through a users' club. There is also output from the Treasury economic model every quarter which is available to Library staff. A decision to make this service permanent has now been taken. It is an interesting example of the possible extension of Library services.

CATALOGUING AND INDEXING

Before 1945 the books and pamphlets which were catalogued had their entries impeccably printed and then carefully stuck into an old interleaved printed catalogue. This method continued until and indeed throughout the Second World War. Similarly, before 1955, official papers, including the papers of the House of Commons itself, were carefully registered in a copperplate hand by the Chief Office Clerk and meticulously filed away for use - if necessary. At this time there was one telephone for incoming calls, not in the Library itself of course, but in a corridor outside, and there were just five senior staff.

The situation with regard to the catalogue changed when the long-established printed catalogue was closed in 1945. The entire Library was then recatalogued on to 3×5 in cards and a system of arrangement of books and of subject indexing based on that of the London Library was introduced. A name catalogue and a separate subject catalogue were started and the headings of the London Library Subject Index were adopted and adapted for use in the alphabetical subject catalogue, and so it has remained to this day. It is true that there are sub-libraries arranged differently: the pamphlet collection, for instance, is classified on a letter and number system; the statistical library perhaps not surprisingly on a system of numbers; and the Scientific Section library by UDC; but the main library, which until the end of the Second World

War certainly overlapped to a great degree with the materials in the London Library, was rearranged in the same order as that great collection.

In 1955, when Roneo strip panels were less commonplace than they are today, they were examined by Mr David Holland (later Librarian 1967–76) with a view to using them to hold a new index of all the papers laid before the House of Commons, the debates and statements in *Hansard*, the detailed chronology of Bills going through Parliament and certain other papers. Increasingly this material was being asked for at short notice and its growing quantity meant that the days of copperplate registers were numbered. What was to be called the Parliamentary Index was born.

Today it has celebrated its silver jubilee, and although sheer volume has led to the chronology of legislation being removed to a separate Bill Index and indexing is more detailed, the principle of compilation is unchanged. Every two years the index is photocopied and bound up and the Roneo panels are then stripped down ready for another two sessions to be added. The Bill Index, which is smaller, we try to keep going for each Parliament or even longer if there is no change of government.

The Parliamentary and later the Bill Indexes were such a success that it was unlikely that the new visible strip indexing system would stop there. Within a few years a Home (i.e. UK) Affairs Index was started which included various departmental press notices, COI publications, longer daily and weekly press comment, departmental circulars and periodical articles etc., which totalled about 15 000 entries a year. Then the International Affairs Section began a similar index, including not only the press etc., but also, selectively, UN, Council of Europe, OECD and many other intergovernmental organization materials. The indexing of Parliamentary Questions followed. Later, the Scientific Section started an index and since 1 January 1973 we have had both a European Communities Index and a separate European Secondary Legislation Index. The latter supplies a chronology of European Commission proposals, monitoring them as they pass through the European Parliament and through the Parliament at Westminster, in the same way as the progress of UK legislation is followed on the Bill Index.

Finally, there is the Chairman's Index on which as far as possible the Library keeps up with the establishment of committees, commissions, working parties etc. which are set up under official auspices and which are not connected with Parliament. Ideally the information includes the date it was set up, its parent department, terms of reference and membership, and its secretary and telephone number. Later a watch is kept for reports on its work, and finally its own report or reports together with their history. The sources for this Index are less easy to define than for the other indexes. It is probably the most subtle to compile.

These combined visible strip indexes now have something like 80 000 entries a year and as only about 5 000 items a year are catalogued it is clear the vital role they play in the Library's work. These indexes enable staff to respond to Members' requests and to control part of the flood of material which arrives and which for obvious reasons is not being indexed on a commercial basis. Even if they were listed in published indexes, these would arrive rather too late.

The indexes were all started by different people at different times so that some years ago their lay-out was standardized and recently a thesaurus has been prepared of 6–7000 terms which will be introduced as these indexes are transferred to a computer-based system beginning in 1980. The use of a computer system will enable this indexing work to be used not just at one or two locations in the Library as at present, but, with the help of VDUs, throughout Parliament and possibly further afield. Those of us who have grown up with these visible strip indexes will be interested to see how the new technology matches up, but what is certain is that with a growing staff and busier Library, it would be quite impossible to multiply the present manual system to meet all the demand. It would be too labour intensive and hence in the long run too expensive.

Until now, an attempt has been made to arrange their work so that indexers and cataloguers spend only part of their time doing this work. They are also engaged in reference work and by that means those who contribute to the indexes are also those who frequently use them. This means that your shortcomings as an indexer or cataloguer may well rebound on you or, if on your colleagues, that you are quite likely to hear about it! It also keeps the indexers alert to the changing problems and definitions to which the index is trying to respond.

LIBRARY OUTPUT

Having set down some account of the role of the Library, its organization and staff and the materials it takes and indexes, etc., it is time to ask the key question – what comes out of the Library?

Compared with most Parliamentary libraries the relationship between Members and the Library staff at the House of Commons is a close one. This is partly because the Library itself is very close to the Chamber (see frontispiece), an easy place to drop in on. It is also a place where you can write letters or speeches, browse in books and journals, or just relax in an armchair. It is a large suite of rooms, two of them with no staff, where Members can get away from everyone except their colleagues. And these respect the tradition of quiet that hangs over the very name Library. Although the increasing personal accommodation for Members means that they probably spend less time in the Library during the office day than, say, fifteen years ago, it is still at the crossroads of the House of Commons and to visit it once or twice a day presents no time-wasting difficulty.

The second factor affecting the use of the Library is the strange pattern of Members' lives. From midday Monday to Friday, or anyway late Thursday night, they are very closely attached to the Palace of Westminster itself. Their Library therefore becomes the source for many small pieces of information, not just major pieces of research. It may be necessary to plan a journey abroad or brief yourself for such a visit, to plan entertainment, to catch up on specialist reading, and to have to do all this within the confines of the Houses of Parliament.

The result of both these factors is that there is a great deal of face-to-face reference work. First, this may concern happenings in Parliament itself, a complicated institution on which to keep detailed tabs. Second, it may concern the government's administration, from great crises to the administration of ploughing grants. Third, there is the nationalized industry sector and the private sector with one member of staff specializing in company information. The welfare state is an important subject as its administration figures in constituency mail.

Most of these subjects would be handled, initially anyway, at a general reference level. Either orally or by putting out selected materials for the Member, a great number of such enquiries will be handled in a week. It should be emphasized that apart from leaflets on the welfare state, and the book-lending scheme, the Library does not supply Members with copies of papers etc. That is the job of the Vote Office. It is obvious that great pressure would be put on the Library by outside organizations, including government departments, if it became accepted that the Library was an agent of distribution of material to Members.

This reference work covers four main areas, namely, Parliament in the Oriel Room, UK matters in the Reference Room, International Affairs in 'A' Room, and European Community matters also in 'A' Room. An extensive press-cuttings service is offered covering these subject areas, but at the present time because of lack of staff the Library is unable to offer Members a Selective Dissemination of Information service.

Moving on from this general reference work, we come to specialist reference work. In 'C' Room of the Library most Research Sections have a desk manned during the day. Here a Member may discuss a problem with more specialist staff. It may be that this is as far as he will want to take the matter, but if he wants a written reply then this will be undertaken by one of these five Research Division Subject Sections. The reply will be in the form of a personal letter to the Member and will be confidential to him. Apart from the fact that Members mostly wish to feel that the reply they get is quite personal to them, experience has taught us that the motive behind the question is very seldom exactly the same in two cases and that while data in a reply is factual, the context is normally political. Of course the staff do not enter into the party political situation, but anyone working for Members would be foolish to ignore the politics which are the background to all their work. Over 4500 of these tailored letters go to Members each year and about 20 per cent are statistical in content and are prepared within the Statistics Section. Of the enquiries answered by the Research Division 98 per cent are for Members.

The time allowed for the preparation of these replies is normally very short. The reasons for this are human enough. First Members are very busy people and tend to tackle a problem near their own deadline. Second, they are very often using the data in a public arena and therefore it is very important not to be out of date. And so they place the question and want the reply at the last moment. It used to be thought that the written answers to about half these enquiries were needed within two or three days and it may well be of that order today. What type of enquiry is getting a written answer?

In 1975 the Library, when giving evidence to the Select Committee on Assistance to Private Members,[11] gave a specimen week's work. About 135 enquiries for written answers had been received and were listed for the Select Committee and a random selection of a dozen or so of these, together with the Subject Section which replied, will give an idea of the variety of output.

Economic Affairs

Background to disagreement between British Leyland and suppliers of components.

Buses, material on bus transport, including licensing.

Home and Parliamentary Affairs

Reorganization of the NHS; impact on social workers.

National Insurance contributions; position of agencies.

Inquiries into broadcasting and the press.

International Affairs

Selection and translation of relevant German poll on public attitudes to the police, 1968.

Political situation in Chile since Allende's overthrow.

Scientific Section

Comment on WEU draft report on nuclear power.

Background to US Project Independence.

Parliamentary activity since 1966 on medical ethics.

Statistical Section

Meaning of the real rate of interest and how to compute the effective interest rate on a particular loan.

The increase in two different concepts of money supply.

M1 and M2 over three 12-month periods.

So far, mention has been made of the individual enquiry. Most of these come from Members themselves, many by a personal visit and discussion, sometimes by letter and sometimes by telephone. The growing number of Members' personal staff, however, has led to more enquiries being filtered through a third person. Obviously, as with all information work at second hand, this can cause problems, especially as questions became more specialized or detailed. Library staff prefer to learn of Members' needs from them direct.

A further but different area of Library output is its anticipatory work. This is information which is gathered together and written up because in the experience of Library staff, Members will be asking for it or would be pleased to have access to it. The starting point for this anticipatory work is a careful examination of the Queen's Speech when she opens a session of Parliament. Here is to be found the Government's initial proposals for Parliament's work for that session. The Research Division Subject Sections assess the Bills and subjects which will be raised in their areas with a view to preparing papers on them in advance. A second basis for this work is when a clutch of enquiries suggests that a problem is coming forward and that it would be more efficient and more satisfactory for a member of the Library staff to examine the subject in great detail and prepare a more comprehensive paper which, even if it does not answer questions on all aspects of the subject, will, after the Member has read it, make it easier for him to place clearer, specific questions.

Most anticipatory work takes the form of Reference Sheets or Background Papers. Some years ago the Research Division just compiled Reference Sheets, which were lists of references normally on a current Bill or subject interesting Parliament. Much of the preliminary work has been done by the various visible strip indexes so it was a question of assembling references from these into intelligent groupings and then most of the material referred to was brought together in boxes. The Member, therefore, had his sources worked out and drawn together for him and he could examine the material, discuss it with the member of staff who had made the compilation, and possibly refine his search further. As Library staff specialized further, increasingly the groups of references in these Reference Sheets became interspersed with comment and sometimes analysis. Shortly after this a few staff members who had had to get to grips with a subject over a period of time decided to write it up, almost in essay form and made it available to Members. Thus was born the Background Paper.

Today both types of paper are brought out and they may be prepared either by one member of staff or even two or three. The list for 1977–8 and early 1978–9 suggests the coverage.

Reference Sheets
Session 1977–8

Offshore Oil and Gas: Government Control (2.11.77)
Scotland Bill [Bill 1 of 1977–8]; Wales Bill [Bill 2 of 1977–8] (9.11.77)
Transport Bill [Bill 43 of 1977–8] (17.1.78)
Protection of Children Bill [Bill 16 of 1977–8] (2.2.78)
Medical Bill [HL] (9.2.78)
Windscale Inquiry Report (16.3.78)
The 1978 Defence Statement (22.3.78)
Nuclear Safeguards and Electricity (Finance) Bill [Bill 96 of 1977–8] (19.4.78)
Back to Square Two... or the Choice of Britain's Next Nuclear Reactor (25.4.78)

Session 1978–9

European Monetary Union (27.10.78)
The Bingham Report: a background bibliography (1.11.78)
Public Lending Right Bill [Bill 5 of 1978–9] (7.11.78)
Nurses, Midwives & Health Visitors' Bill [Bill 3 of 1978–9] (9.11.78)
Companies Bill [Bill 2 of 1978–9] (9.11.78)

House of Commons (Redistribution of Seats) Bill [Bill 6 of 1978–9] (14.11.78)
Social Security Bill [Bill 8 of 1978–9] (14.11.78)
Banking Bill [Bill 7 of 1978–9] (21.11.78)
The Rate Support Grant Settlement 1978–9 (22.11.78)
Merchant Shipping Bill [Bill 13 of 1978–9] (28.11.78)
Education Bill [Bill 14, of 1978–9] (29.11.78)
Official Secrets and Open Government (8.1.79)
Vaccine Damage Payments Bill [Bill 58 of 1978–9] (1.2.79)
Crown Agents Bill [Bill 61 of 1977–8] (5.2.79)
Vandalism (7.2.79)
Independence for the Gilbert Islands: the Kiribati Bill (Bibliography) [HL]
   (15.2.79)
Road Traffic (Seat Belts) Bill 1979 (16.2.79)

Background Papers

By-election Results since the General Election of October 1974 (13.6.77)
Special Measures to Alleviate Unemployment in Great Britain (29.6.77)
Statistics of Defence (18.11.77)
The Devolution Debate: Regional Statistics (Updated) (8.3.78)
By-election Results since General Election of October 1974 (Updated)
   (6.12.78)
Labour Relations Legislation (30.1.79)
Emergency Powers (22.1.79)
The Devolution Question: Regional Statistics (20.2.79)

Although staff do not, of course, inject politics into these papers – this is left to
the Members themselves – this does not mean to say that there need be anything
anaemic about them. The crisis in the financial arrangements of the Crown
Agents, for instance, certainly hit the headlines in 1977 and Bill 61 of session
1978–9 attempted to remedy the problem. In the Reference Sheet prepared for
the Bill it is clear that there is some gusto in an introductory paragraph which
reads as follows:

> The saga of the Crown Agents' own-account dealings, and the role in them of
> some of their staff, has been very fully documented in much of the material
> included in this Reference Sheet, particularly in the Fay Report, and it is not
> proposed to repeat it here. The list of companies in which the Crown Agents
> invested reads now like a roll-call of the more spectacular failures of the property
> and secondary banking sectors in the early 1970s. In fairness, it does have to be
> pointed out that in the late 1960s investment in such enterprises was widely
> regarded as a perfectly respectable financial practice, even if the track record of
> the Crown Agents was subsequently so conspicuous for their success in picking
> losers rather than winners. In addition, the many critics of their activities never
> seriously argued that the objective of building up reserves was wrong in itself.
> What was wrong was how it was done.[12]

The sources used for these Reference Sheets and Background Papers are mostly a wide range of official papers, including statistics, authoritative political publications, journal articles and press comment, pressure group literature, etc. To these must be added any earlier Parliamentary history and the law, if any, as it stands. The spectrum of sources is up to the compiler.

Some of these papers may be quite long, 30–40 pages, and represent very useful contributions to the subjects themselves. The House of Commons Library does not make them available to outsiders, but copies are sent to Aslib and to the European Centre for Parliamentary Research and Documentation at Luxembourg. Aslib list them in *Aslib Information* and the European Centre in their newsletter and both will supply photocopies on request. And although the Library cannot offer Selective Dissemination of Information services to Members individually, the Reference Sheets and Reference Boxes of material which go with them, are both updated daily, especially when the Bill they cover is going through both Houses of Parliament.

Finally, in this group of anticipatory papers there are Research Notes. These are short analytical pieces prepared quickly to meet urgent demand. They are made available to Members and Peers but are not sent outside the Houses of Parliament. Normally they are on narrow subjects such as an individual industrial dispute or a particular aspect of social welfare such as the 'Housewives non-contributory invalidity pension' where the Statutory and Regulation background is lucidly explained together with its Parliamentary history.

Library staff's contribution to the work of Select Committees over the years has been spasmodic. At times two or three Library Clerks have been helping subject committees but the tradition has always been for the Select Committee to have its own staff, a Clerk, and, in recent years, maybe a Specialist Adviser who is dedicated to serving the Committee only. In evidence to the Select Committee on Assistance to Private Members in 1975 the Library suggested among future developments that there might be:

> a pool of research staff, based on the Library, who could be seconded full-time to the service of Committees as and when they were needed. Such a scheme would have the following advantages:
> (a)   the continuity imparted by permanent staff with experience of previous Select Committee enquiries;
> (b)   the undivided loyalties of staff permanently serving the House of Commons;
> (c)   the Library would be able to employ such staff on other duties at such times as they were not employed by Committees.[13]

In the subsequent Report[14] the Select Committee did not take up this point and the Select Committee on Procedure Report[15] some years later, which spent considerable time examining the need to reform the Select Committee system and made far-reaching proposals for changes, including staffing, restricted its comments on the Library's role to the following:

> Select committees are free to seek assistance from the House of Commons

Librarian and his staff when their expertise would be of particular relevance to a committee's inquiries. The Library provides the only existing pool of full-time expert staff directly under the control of the House and although relatively small in numbers these staff can be of considerable assistance to Members in locating and analysing published material on a wide range of subjects. This expertise can be put to valuable use in providing background material for select committees, particularly at the beginning of new inquiries, on the lines of the Background Notes and similar papers on issues of current interest prepared by the Library for the use of Members generally. We believe that select committees should make more use of these services, but it would not be right for such assistance to be provided at the expense of the Library's services to individual Members.[16]

What are Members' views of the Library's work? The fullest analysis of this question was undertaken by Anthony Barker and Michael Rush at the end of the 1960s.[17] There is an attempt to analyse Members' appreciation of Reference services and Research services, but without an adequate attempt to define them – a task which would seem very difficult. More recently, in a series of interesting letters from Members sent to the Select Committee on Assistance to Private Members,[18] many of them set down their need for better Library services. At the time of writing this report had not been considered by the House. On a day-to-day basis Members both orally, and in letters, express appreciation of work done for them and this is sometimes made plain in speeches in the House. It is clear, of course, that occasionally they are not satisfied, when they are equally articulate! Maybe the best touchstone however, is that they 'ask for more', not only in quantity but also quality and this supplies the appreciation which the staff needs.

A LIBRARY DAY

Maybe the Library day can be said to start when a busy group of green-coated cleaners work their way through the Library very early in the morning emptying the ample wastepaper baskets. Out goes yesterday's information – except that the Library will have kept a copy of important material for future needs.

The next sound – the telephones are still quiet at this hour and the day staff have yet to arrive – will be the noise of electric cleaners as the Library's small team of cleaners start their work of dusting the books on the shelves.

By 9 a.m. the first deliveries of mail are being sorted, the day's newspapers filed and the first Parliamentary Papers are arriving. The 'Vote' and *Hansard* have just come in, straight from St Stephen's Press, and they are being delivered to staff desks. A few Members are coming in with their morning's mail, including some from constituents, points from which they may later wish to discuss with specialist Library staff.

Half an hour later the senior staff begin to arrive and their first job is to pick up urgent enquiries left by colleagues a few hours earlier, enquiries from Members who were in the House the previous night and who will be in for the answers very shortly. They have an early appointment with a Minister, an official or a pressure group. The first 'phone goes, a Member checking on something before meeting a civil servant or local government official at 10 a.m., and then several Members arrive together. They are on their way to a Standing Committee examining a Bill which starts at 10.30 a.m. and they cannot wait for their answers which they want sent up to the committee room on the floor above. One of them is going straight from the Standing Committee, which will continue until 1 p.m., to a lunch at a foreign embassy and he would like a note on a visiting statesman and the present state of his country sent to the committee room for him to read before lunch.

The first distribution of material from government departments, press notices, circulars, pamphlets, etc. arrive mid-morning together with a second or third delivery of mail. And the staff who were on duty the previous night will be back so that the staff, and hence subject specialization, are again at full strength. (House of Commons staff working for Members do not take leave during the Parliamentary session in order to sustain the service they need when the House is sitting.)

By midday, Members may have worked out the enquiries which they wish to make or the discussion they wish to have with Library staff as a result of their mail. They may fit this in before lunch. Those not on Standing Committees may only now be arriving from meetings and other duties and if there is going to be an important vote and they have been summoned by a three-line whip, then the numbers who will be around by lunch-time may be considerable.

The half-hour before Question Time starts at 2.30 p.m. will be a brisk one with Members checking last-minute points for their supplementary questions to Ministers or for the debate which follows. If after Question Time a Minister is going to make a statement in the House, he may well deposit special embargoed papers in the Library in advance. Once the Minister has sat down, a wave of Members will leave the chamber to seek these documents and maybe related information.

About tea-time final deliveries of mail arrive, together with the last distribution of documents from government departments and HMSO, and these coincide with the evening papers and a reduction of telephone calls. A subtle but important change is taking place and by 6 p.m. the cycle of the office day is ending. Members, who increasingly have office space and personal staff outside the Palace of Westminster, are leaving these and returning to the Palace itself. Government departments and other offices are closing down. At this time the day staff go home and there remain the dozen or so who are on that night's duty. The Library has become isolated in the national information network and at the same time it is becoming increasingly used by Members themselves.

The House of Commons as a club is reasserting itself and this, of course, changes the atmosphere of its Library. During the day both Members and staff have been under pressures from outside that disappear in the evening and the consequent relaxation can result in a richer dialogue between them. Questions can be placed, material browsed through or borrowed, staff consulted at leisure. There are aesthetic touches too: the whiff of a good cigar after dinner, the sprinkling of dinner-jackets as Members returning from formal dinner parties get back in time for the vote at 10 p.m.

And after the division, another wave of Members may well arrive in the Library and if they are required by the business of the House to stay later it would be quite normal for 80 or more of them to be working and reading in the Library at 11 p.m. or later. The Library can seat about 90 Members.

Finally, the House will start on the last half-hour adjournment debate and the staff will clear up the Library in readiness for the next day or more likely for later the same day. And when they have left any important messages for their colleagues arriving in the morning, helped a few Members who have left their enquiries until the last moment, heard the bells ringing as the Speaker rises to adjourn the House, they certainly will respond to the echo down the corridors of the policeman's call 'Who goes home?'.

There is no typical Library day. There are some comparatively fixed aspects to the work, e.g. the Library is open about 15 hours on an average sitting day and the quantity of documentation and indeed enquiries continues to grow steadily. There are also quite unpredictable aspects such as the current political atmosphere, the relations between the Government and the House of Commons, the sudden crisis at home or abroad. Somewhere in the middle of all these tensions the staff find their personal challenge.

THE FUTURE

The cut-off date for this work is mid-1980 and anything which may happen after that date is termed the future. It is certain that any changes or developments which take place will be those required by the House of Commons itself and that, for the next decade anyway, one of the great restraints will be the lack of staff accommodation, indeed all accommodation, at Westminster.

The Services Committee report on House of Commons information for the public recommended the development of the Sale Office in the Vote Office into a proper bookshop for the sale of official Parliamentary material to the public. When it happens, and accommodation is one of the difficulties delaying its introduction, it will be closely linked to the new Information Office situated in the Library Department. It is clearly more efficient for both these services to be in the same Department and working closely together. The same report recommended the establishment of an educational service, specifically for schools, and the recent appointment of an Education Officer who will cover school visits to both the House of Commons and the House of Lords means that this service will start in the financial year 1980–81. Finally, this Report suggested that the 'House Returns', i.e. the annual returns to the House of Commons about its work covering Public Bills, Committee Work, days and hours of sitting, etc., should be worked up into an annual paper which should be published, probably as a House of Commons paper, and this is now being planned. These three proposals will complete action on the Select Committee's ideas for improving information for the public.

Looking a little further ahead the picture lacks clear definition. The Library has expressed its view in evidence to the Services Committee that the introduction of computer-based indexing, once it has been fully established, may mean that much of this database, provided the priority of service to Members was not affected, might become a public service.

The external picture is also changing. 1979 saw the direct election of a European Parliament. Already a network of correspondents for co-operation between Parliamentary libraries in the Nine (indeed it covers all members of the Council of Europe) exists, working with the European Centre of Parliamentary Research and Documentation in the European Parliament at Luxembourg. The working group on co-operation between Parliamentary libraries is chaired from Westminster. The objective of these correspondents is to improve the sharing and the transfer of information as national parliaments adjust their role in a more integrated Europe, especially following the creation of a directly elected European Parliament. The method is severely practical with its minimum of overheads. The House of Commons and its Library in particular is therefore becoming increasingly part of a new network of information as many decisions which affect us as citizens are hatched and taken in Brussels, as well as in Whitehall.

The implications of this particular change are difficult to judge but a Select Committee of the House of Lords has looked at this question in connection with the directly elected European Parliament.[19]

Among the new needs they anticipate is the exchange of information, in particular between the British Members of the European Parliament and Members of the Westminster Parliament. It is clear that there are demarcations between the interests and responsibilities of Members (Luxembourg) MEPs and Members (Westminster) MPs which will be quite complicated. The House of Commons has considered whether MEPs may use certain House of Commons Library facilities to help them meet this new challenge.

So far Library developments which have either been decided in principle or which are needed to meet external changes have been mentioned.

It happens that there is a paper on the Library's future on the table. That is, there is a Select Committee report which spells out proposals for the Library's future. As yet, it has not been considered by the House. The recommendations in summary form as as follows:

> the doubling of the research service [which, spelt out, means] twelve additional senior staff (Library Clerks and above, most of them subject specialists), plus six supporting staff, would be needed in order to approximately double the research services as they were in January 1975 ... [and] ... these increases would need to be accompanied by some expansion of the reference and supporting Library staff in the Parliamentary Division, e.g. possibly eight extra staff, of whom the majority would belong to the clerical and junior grades.

This was described by the Committee as a modest recommendation. In addition they advocated that a review of the operation of the expanded Library service should be undertaken within three or four years of the implementation of this recommendation.[20]

During the last few years the House of Commons's domestic interests have focused on new accommodation, the reform of the administration of the House culminating in the House of Commons Administration Act 1978, and consideration of the question of the reform of procedure. It will be of interest to see, especially following the introduction of Departmental Select Committees, whether their interest during the early 1980s will again return to their own Library's services.

Finally there is the science fiction (rapidly become fact) aspect of the future. Already the Library takes video tapes of broadcasts from the various regions in order to keep Members who have to be at Westminster informed about constituency as well as national problems. The House of Commons Information Office is contributing to the Post Office Prestel system of information distribution via the domestic TV screen and a Prestel set is available to Members in their Library suite. The Library provides Members with help concerning access to the Treasury Economic Model which may prove to be a significant extension to Members' information in debating economic policy. In the future, computer power, whether an aspect of new routines at Westminster or providing new sources of information from outside, e.g. the introduction of Euronet including various official European Community databases, is certainly going to set a challenge to the flexibility and indeed the imagination of House of Commons Library staff.

Whatever the future, deadlines for Members at Westminster will remain tight, accuracy of information as essential as up-to-dateness, and the range of interests stretch to the past for precedents and to the future for invention. Any technical innovation which will really help Members and their staff to understand what is happening in the present and how it is shaping the future will have to be assessed and its potential turned to advantage.

BIBLIOGRAPHY AND PRINTED CATALOGUES

The Bibliography that follows is made up of Official Reports by the House of Commons on its Library or where Library matters were important. It reflects the early years of activity, followed by nearly a century of inactivity and then the post-war progress. The Printed Catalogues also reflect early activity, the pause for a generation after the 1834 fire, and the second spate of activity during and after moving into the new Library in the middle of the nineteenth century. The last full printed catalogue was printed in 1910.

Official Reports
Report from the Select Committee appointed to inquire into the state and condition of the Printed Reports and other Papers presented, to consider of providing some proper place for the safe custody of the Printed Books and Papers, and who were also instructed to consider the best means of providing additional accommodation for Committee-rooms with the least possible

delay   1825 (496) v.7
Second Report from the same   1825 (515) v.11
Third Report from the same   1825 (516) v.21
Report from the Select Committee appointed to inquire into the present state of
the Library of the House of Commons, to consider respecting future
Regulations for the preservation and management thereof; 1830 (496) iv.25
Report from the Select Committee appointed in the following Session to
consider the same subject   1831-32 (600) v.245
Report from the Select Committee on Official Houses, to whom the Report
which was made on 7th July instant, from the Select Committee on the Library
of the House of Commons, was referred   1834 (480) xi.449
Report from the Standing Committee appointed to assist Mr Speaker in the
direction of the Library   1834 (463) xi.329
Report from the Standing Committee appointed in the following Session for the
same purpose   1835 (104) xviii.105
Report from the Standing Committee appointed in the following Session for the
same purpose   1836 (63) xxi.97
Report from the Standing Committee appointed in the following Session for the
same purpose   1837 (468) xiii.65
Report from the Standing Committee appointed in the following Session for the
same purpose   1837-38 (691) xxiii.499
Report from the Standing Committee appointed in the following Session for the
same purpose   1839 (406) xiii.1
Report from the Standing Committee on the Library of The House;
                                                                   1841 (422) ix.597
Report from the Standing Committee appointed in a subsequent Session on the
same subject   1845 (610) xii.465
Report from the Standing Committee appointed in a subsequent Session on the
same subject   1852 (453) v.441
Reports of Standing Committee appointed to assist Mr Speaker
                                                                   1856 (426) vii.569
Report from the Standing Committee on the Library of the House of Commons
with the proceedings of the Committee   1857 (Session 1) (123) ii.731
Standing Committees were set up until 1861 but no further Reports were made.
On 18 July 1922 the first meeting of the Committee appointed to advise and
assist Mr Speaker in the management of the Library was held. This Committee
continued until 1965 when it was replaced by the Library Sub-Committee of
the new House of Commons (Services) Committee. The Advisory Committee
published only one Report, 10th Special Report   1960-61 (246) vi.273
Special Report from the Select Committee on Library (House of Commons)
together with Minutes of Proceedings, Evidence and Appendices
                                                                   1944-5 (98) ii.345
First and Second Reports from the Select Committee on the Library (House of
Commons) with Minutes of Proceedings, Minutes of Evidence and
Appendix   1945-6 (35, 99-2) viii.33

Report from the Select Committee on House of Commons Accommodation, etc, together with Minutes and Evidence (includes oral and written evidence from the Library) 1952-3 (309) vi.23

1953-4 (184) vii.5

Second Report (of the Estimates Committee) with part of the evidence taken before Sub-Committee E and Appendices on the House of Commons Library 1960-61 (168) v.171

Tenth Special Report (Observations of Mr Speaker's Advisory Committee) on the Report (of the Estimates Committee) on the House of Commons Library; 1960-1 (246) vi.273

Report from the Select Committee on the Palace of Westminster with Proceedings, Minutes of Evidence and Appendices (includes oral and written evidence from the Library) 1964-5 (285) x.343

Review of the Administrative Services of the House of Commons. Report to Mr Speaker by Sir Edmund Compton (includes information on the Library Department) 1974 (254) vi.1115

House of Commons (Administration) Report to Mr Speaker by Committee under the Chairmanship of Mr Arthur Bottomley (includes information on the Library Department) 1974-5 (624) xii.255

Second Report from the Select Committee on Assistance to Private Members: Research Assistance (includes oral and written Evidence from the Library Department) 1974-5 (662) xii.759

Minutes of Evidence and Appendices (includes oral and written Evidence from the Library) 1974-5 (375, 375-i) xii.775

Report of the Informal Joint Committee on Computers to the Leaders of both Houses (includes written evidence from the Library Department);1976-7 (78)

Fifth Report from the Select Committee on House of Commons (Services) with Minutes of Evidence and Appendix: Computer-based indexing for the Library 1976-7 (377)

Eighth Report from the Select Committee on House of Commons (Services) with Minutes of Evidence: Services for the Public (includes oral and written evidence from the Library Department) 1976-7 (509)

Seventh Report from the Select Committee on House of Commons (Services) with Minutes of Evidence and Appendices: Computer applications for the House of Commons (includes oral and written evidence from the Library Department) 1977-8 (617 i and ii)

Printed Catalogues

Catalogue of Books in the Library at the House of Commons 1830
1829-30 HC 80

Alphabetical Catalogue of the Library of the House of Commons (1837-8)
1837-8 HC 691 pp.5-10

Catalogue of the Library of the House of Commons (1852) 1852 88 pp.
Catalogue of the Library of the House of Commons (1853) 1853 106 pp.
Catalogue of the Library of the House of Commons (1856) 1856 305 pp.

An appendix of Catalogue and Tracts and Pamphlets (List of Parliamentary
Collection)
Catalogue of the Library of the House of Commons (1857)   1857 317 pp.
Appendices of collections of pamphlets
Supplement of East India Company Papers;   Reprinted 1889 319-96 pp.
Catalogue of the Books in the Library of the House of Commons with an index
of subjects and an Appendix (1862)   1862 249 pp.
                                                      New ed. 1864 254 pp.
Catalogue of Books in the Library of the House of Commons (1888)1888 316
pp. An index of subjects to the Catalogue of Books in the Library of the House of
Commons (1889)   1889 (no pagination)
Numerical list and index to the East India Papers presented by the East India
Company to the Library of the House of Commons (1861)   1861 189 pp.
Catalogue of the Books in the Library of the House of Commons (1910)
                                                             1910 351 pp.
                                    Supplements 1920, 1930 and 1943

Personal Research Assistants

It was as recently as 1969 that the House of Commons agreed that their
Members might claim, if they used it, £500 a year secretarial allowance. In 1971
when the Boyle Committee proposed that the allowance should be doubled it
indicated that £300 might be used to pay a research assistant.

During 1971 a survey was made of some 386 Members, excluding Ministers,
and already 10 per cent of these had research assistants. The two factors which
have limited the growth of the number of research assistants have been finance
and accommodation but the situation with regard to both has improved in
recent years. By mid-1980 the allowance had gone up to £6,750 a year which
can be divided between secretarial and/or research assistant allowance as the
Member sees fit and additional accommodation, some of it specifically for
research assistants, became available with the opening of the Norman Shaw
(North) building in 1975.

The 1970s therefore have seen the introduction of a new link in the
information chain for Members. This fact confirms the analysis of Members'
wishes carried out as long ago as 1966 by Barker and Rush who found that then
some 35 per cent of those Members questioned expressed a wish for a personal
research assistant.[21]

It is difficult for research assistants to work for their Member without
adequate sources. For this reason, the Library Sub-Committee as soon as the
research assistants were figures on the Parliamentary landscape, started to
allow them limited access to certain Library facilities. By 1978 this access at
restricted times and to limited places was permitted to 150 research assistants. It
is a difficult balance to establish as the privacy of the Members' Library is very
important to them.

In 1975, when a branch library was opened in the newly acquired and renovated Norman Shaw (North) building, it was possible to offer a good library service there not only to Members but also to their secretaries and research assistants and this throughout the day and during most of the year and without restriction. This represented an important step forward in the facilities available for the personal staff of Members.

In 1974 a Select Committee was set up 'to examine the present support facilities available to Private Members... in particular research assistance on matters before Parliament and to make recommendations for such improvements as they consider necessary'.[22] The Committee took evidence from officials of the House including Library staff. They established the work of research assistants as having a 'political dimension' which Library staff 'would not wish to provide'. They recommended that the provision of research assistants to any Member who wanted them should be additional to a full-time secretary and that although they should be centrally paid they should be 'personal to the individual Member'. This report was made to the House in October 1975 but so far no formal action has been taken on it. But Members' personal research assistants are a new fact of life at Westminster and their use of House of Commons Library facilities is increasing.

One of the problems with regard to research assistants is that many of them do not stay very long, sometimes a session, sometimes only a few months but seldom for years. There is, of course, no career progression for them and so the permanent staff of the House, including Library staff, are frequently having to explain the pattern and techniques of Parliamentary information to newcomers. These may be youngsters on their way to university or recent graduates or people with aspirations towards a political career who hope to learn from such practical experience. (At the 1979 general election, nine candidates who had held positions as Members' research assistants were elected as MPs.) There can be little doubt that they increase the amount of work that Library staff must undertake but it is equally clear that for many Members they meet a very real need. It will be interesting to follow how the idea of research assistants develops during the 1980s.

Notes

1 April 1980 figure.
2 Since April 1980 the Refreshment Department has formed a sixth Department.
3 Scottish Grand Committee considers certain Bills and Estimates and the Welsh Grand Committee certain Bills. The House of Commons occasionally refers Bills to Standing Committees for the second reading debate.
4 Young, A. *Tour of Ireland.* 1780, 1.
5 *Special Report for the Select Committee on Library* (H of C) 1944–45 (98) II. Appendix A. 1.
6 *Second Report for the Estimates C'ttee on the House of Commons Library* 1960–1, (168) V, Evidence, 1–2.

7 See *Memorandum of Guidance for Officals appearing before Select C'ttees* Appendix D of 1st Report from Sel. C'ttee on Procedure 1977–8 (HC 588-I).

8 *First and Second Reports from the Sel. C'ttee on House of Commons Library* 1945-6 (35, 99-2) VIII. 33 para. 5.

9 *Second Report of the Estimates Committee on the House of Commons Library* 1960-1 (168) V. 171.

10 *Tenth Special Report on the House of Commons Library* 1960-1 (246) VI. 273.

11 1974-5 (375, 375-I) XII, 779-806.

12 House of Commons Library Reference Sheet 79/3, Crown Agents Bill, p.2.

13 1974-5 (375, 375-I) XII, 786.

14 1974-5 (662) XII, 759.

15 1977-8 HC 588-I *First Report from the Select Committee on Procedure.*

16 1977-8 HC 588-I p.lxxxii.

17 See Barker, A. and Rush, M. The Member of Parliament and his Information 1970 pp.305-26.

18 1974-5 (375, 375-1.) XII, 875-887.

19 *Relations between the UK Parliament and the European Parliament after direct elections.* 1977-8 HL (256-1.)

20 *Second report from the Select Committee on Assistance to Private Members.* 1974-5. (662) XII 763-4.

21 Barker, A. and Rush, M. The Member of Parliament and his Information 1970, p.326.

22 *Select Committee on Assistance to Private Members evidence* 1974-5 (375, 375-i) XII 775-896: *Second Report from the Select Committee on Assistance to Private Members* 1974-5 (662) XII 759-773.

CHAPTER TWO

House of Lords

The Organization

MEMBERS

The membership of the House of Lords is much larger than that of the House of Commons. It also varies from time to time. In June 1980 it included 26[1] Archbishops and Bishops, 766 hereditary peers, 17 Life peers created under the Appellate Jurisdiction Act and 319 Life peers. Of these, some 80 have not received a writ of summons and may not take their seats and 178 have obtained leave of absence. There have been no hereditary peers created since 1965. The Life Peerage Act 1958, introducing Life peers who are created on the recommendation of the Prime Minister, has greatly changed the active element in the House of Lords. The average daily attendance in 1978-9 was 292, for which attendance peers may claim expenses in addition to travel within a maximum of £36 a day. Peers receive no allowance for secretarial or research assistance. Of this average daily attendance of 282, the Life peers' element is strong.

There has been no real attempt to analyse the professions of peers nor their interests. *Lords on the Board* by A Roth attempts to list Directorships etc., under broad categories, but there is no tabulated analysis such as exists for the House of Commons in the *Times Book of the House of Commons*.

Members of the House of Lords run the services of their House through the large House of Lords Offices Committee with about sixty peers on it. This has similar Sub-Committees to the House of Commons (Services) Committee covering Administration, Finance, the Library, the Refreshment Department, Staff of the House, and Works of Art. Recently a Sub-Committee on Computers was appointed.

STAFF

The staff of the House of Lords numbers 200 who are divided among four Departments: those of the Chairman of Committees, the Clerk of the Parliaments, whose staff is known collectively as the Parliament Office, the Library and Black Rod; staff assisting the Librarian are appointed by the Clerk of the Parliaments.

It is the House of Lords Offices Committee which recommends to the House

From an original drawing by Peter Heaton

STRANGERS' GALLERY

The Chamber of the House of Lords

the appointment of the Librarian of the House of Lords, whereas it is the Speaker who appoints the Librarian of the House of Commons.

The office of the Chairman of Committees, who has general Supervision over Private Bills, Provisional Order Confirmation Bills, and Hybrid Instruments, is small and it need not detain us in the context of this work. Black Rod's Department has very much the same responsibilities to the House of Lords as the Serjeant at Arms and his Department has to the House of Commons. Both are Crown appointments as are the Clerks of both Houses. Black Rod is responsible for security, accommodation and various other services to the House and also as

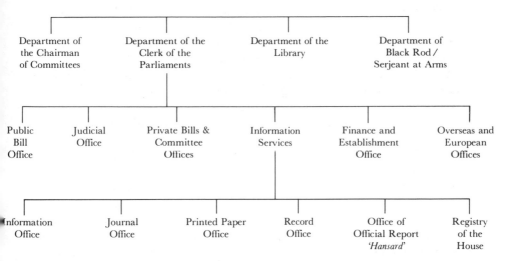

Fig. 2.1   House of Lords staff, organization chart

Secretary to the Lord Great Chamberlain is responsible for certain ceremonial duties and arrangements. Leaving these two Departments aside, together with the post of Librarian the rest of the staff of the House of Lords are centralized in the Parliament Office which is run by the Clerk of the Parliaments.

In 1972 it was decided to create a new post of Principal Clerk, Information Services, and to group under him a series of small Offices which were concerned in one way or another with information for or concerning the House of Lords. The Department of the Library is separate as it is run by the House of Lords Offices Committee of Peers themselves, through a Library sub-committee.

WORK

The House of Lords ordinarily sits on Tuesdays and Wednesdays at 2.30 p.m. and on Thursdays at 3.00 p.m. As the session proceeds and the House of Commons passes Bills which must be considered by the House of Lords, firstly Monday sittings at 2.30 p.m. and later Friday sittings at 11 a.m. are introduced. In recent years the House of Lords has sometimes sat through the evenings until quite late, the average time of rising being 8.20 p.m. The work of the House of Lords is, of course, similar to the House of Commons in many respects, but it is also the Supreme Court of Appeal for civil cases for the United Kingdom and criminal cases for the United Kingdom, excluding Scotland. Only the Lord Chancellor and the Lords of Appeal in ordinary and certain Lords who hold or have held judicial office, take part in its Court of Appeal work. Normally the appeals are heard in a Committee Room and only the judgments are announced in the chamber.

After daily Question Time when the number of Oral Questions is limited to only four, the most time-consuming part of the work of the House of Lords, which in 1977–8 took about 50 per cent of its time, concerns Public Bills. The procedure is essentially the same as the House of Commons, except that the House of Lords hardly ever uses a Public Bill Committee, the equivalent of the Commons Standing Committee, but sits in a Committee of the whole House. Most of the time spent on legislation is spent revising Bills sent from the Commons and because of its legal tradition the House of Lords can do a great deal of tidying up in a detached and rather professional way. About 30 per cent of its time the Lords spends debating reports and general subjects, often far-reaching debates on subjects such as the environment or leisure and they are usually debated in a measured and well-informed way. It is a pity that the House of Lords debates are so seldom used as a source of information in view of the wisdom and experience concentrated there, which comes across without political venom and often with courteous eccentricity. Unstarred Questions, which come at the end of the day, are like short Adjournment Debates in the Commons and take up about 9 per cent of their Lordships' time. Finally, there are the debates on the reports of the House of Lords European Communities Committee, whch has formed seven specialist sub-committees, is manned by about 90 Peers, and is able to devote far more time to the subject than the equivalent House of Commons Select Committee. The House of Lords itself spends nearly 5 per cent of its time debating the European Committee's reports, far more time than the House of Commons can afford. The more important statements made in the House of Commons are usually repeated in the House of Lords.

The Papers

MINUTES OF PROCEEDINGS AND WHITE ORDER PAPER

The Minutes of Proceedings, the equivalent of the House of Commons 'Vote' is headed 'House of Lords', followed by the date in Latin and then the words 'Minutes of Proceedings'. Each daily issue has a serial number and there is continuous pagination through the session. The main parts of the Minutes are:

Yesterday's Business

1   The minutes of the previous day's meeting including a record of reports made, decisions made, papers laid before the House, an account of judicial business conducted that day, and the time of rising and of the next meeting.

2   Judicial Cause Sheet. Details of petitions deposited and appellate committee meetings and judgments.

Notices and Order of the Day

3   Notices of the entire business for the next sitting day. (This is also printed separately as the White Order Paper unpaginated.)

4   Notices of all other business for up to one month ahead.

5   Notices of Motions

    (a)   With No Day Named which to some extent is the equivalent of the House of Commons Early Day Motion.

(b)   Motion for Short Debates. These are balloted for and two are taken each month before Whitsun.

6   Questions for Written answer, which though far less numerous than the House of Commons Questions for Written answer, are increasing.

7   A list of all Bills etc., detailing their progress, which is a daily equivalent of the House of Commons Private Bill List and Public Bill List.

8   A list of future committee meetings with the title of the Committee and the time of Meeting.

The Minutes of the House of Lords are unindexed and are obtainable from HMSO on a subscription basis. They form the basis of part of the House of Lords Journal.

THE JOURNAL

The *Journal* of the House of Lords has the same status as that of the Commons, being the official record of what took place and of the papers laid before the House. However it differs from the Commons *Journal* in that it lists all the peers who have attended on each day; proceedings of the Committee of the Whole House are included; the text of select Committee reports are printed in the *Journal*, though not the Minutes of Proceedings or the Evidence, to find which you must go to the Sessional Papers; the index in each sessional volume is in one part, not two, because the number of papers laid before the House and ordered to be printed is very small – most of them have already been through this procedure with the House of Commons, so they do not need reprinting as House of Lords papers.

The first manuscript journals known date from the early fifteenth century, and the official series at Westminster dates from 1510. It was first printed in the second half of the eighteenth century and it is covered by a series of cumulative indexes, the first six of which covered 1510–1853; they have been published decennially ever since. The latest one covers 1964–1973.

SESSIONAL PAPERS

The Sessional Papers of the House of Lords consists of Bills and House of Lords papers in one numbered sequence throughout the session, the number being printed in the bottom left-hand corner in round brackets (1). There have been no Command papers in the set since 1900 to avoid duplication with the House of Commons Sessional Papers. There is each session a paper called 'Titles and Tables of Contents for the Sessional Papers of the House of Lords'. This is really just a table of contents covering an alphabetical list of Bills, followed by the Papers arranged in broad subjects. Between 1900 and 1921 there was published each session an index which covered the Bills and Papers and also the Command papers but because the latter had been dropped in 1900 it was an index to a non-existing set. After the First World War a typical set of House of Lords Sessional Papers would consist of only four or five volumes. In recent years the position has changed because of the explosion of work undertaken by the House of Lords Select Committee on European Communities. In recent sessions there have been some seven or eight volumes, many of the papers representing the publication of important evidence and views on European Community proposals and affairs. All the papers are, of course, listed in the House of Lords *Journal* and in *Government Publications*, the latter includ ing all the individual Amendment Sheets to Bills and all can be bought as separate items from HMSO. They are not included in BNB.

Quite a number of less important Bills are first introduced into the House of Lords, rather than into the House of Commons. Just as with Commons Bills, immediately after first reading, a formal procedure, the Bills are ordered to be printed and are given a number in round brackets. Amendments to Bills in the House of Lords carry this same number followed by a letter of the alphabet indicating which amendment it is but if Bills are amended in Committee stage or later and reprinted as amended, then they are given new numbers. Further amendments at later stages are similarly lettered after the latest number of the Bill. Let us consider an actual Bill - the Redundancy Payments Bill 1977 - and cover its history and printing in both Houses:

House of Commons
   Stage

1st Reading and order to print		10.3.77
2nd Reading	[Bill 83]	21.3.77
Committee Standing Committee B		
As amended in Standing Committee B	[Bill 103]	5.4.77
Report Stage		5.4.77
3rd Reading		2.5.77

House of Lords

1st Reading and order to print		3.5.77
2nd Reading	(147)	17.5.77
Committee: Amendments	(147a)	21.6.77
As amended in Committee	(188)	21.6.77
Report: Amendments	(188a)	28.6.77
As amended on Report	(209)	28.6.77
3rd Reading		30.6.77

House of Commons

Lords Amendments	[Bill 149]	5.7.77

House of Lords

Commons reasons for disagreeing		
to the Lords Amendments	(225)	6.7.77
Royal Assent	1977, Chapter 22	22.7.77

This rather complicated History shows the different numbering of the House of Commons [Bill-] and House of Lords (-), the way in which legislation shuttles backwards and forwards, the numbering of Lords amendments, a disagreement between the Houses and, finally, the Royal Assent in the House of Lords for the Bill to become a statute with a chapter number.

The Papers of the House of Lords Sessional Papers are all Reports and evidence from Select Committees of the House, and just occasionally Joint Select Committees, in which case the papers are in both House of Commons Sessional Papers and House of Lords Sessional Papers.

The main indexes to the House of Lords Sessional Papers are 1801-59, 1859-70, 1871-84/5, sessionally 1886-1921 and 1922 onwards just a general table of contents.

PARLIAMENTARY DEBATES

House of Lords
There is a daily issue of Parliamentary debates (*Hansard*) for the House of Lords and there is, like the Commons, a weekly index to these debates. In the bound volumes of debates the indexes are cumulated from the beginning of the session. These cumulated volume indexes can be purchased separately. The final cumulation is the sessional index published in the last volume of debates, not as a separate index volume. All the material in the debates is arranged in one numbered sequence.

House of Lords Committees
Public Bill Committees are seldom used in the House of Lords, but when they are the debates are reported in the same way as the Commons Standing Committees. It often takes several sessions to have enough debates to complete a volume and HMSO does not republish them in bound form or publish any kind of index to them (see Table 2.1).

Table 2.1 Table of Papers and Printed Indexes

Title	Frequency	Indexing	Notes
Minutes of Proceedings	Sitting days	No	Those parts reproduced in the Journal are indexed there
Official Report (*Hansard*)	After sitting days	Weekly. Each volume (cumulating through the session)	Index in the volumes cumulates throughout the session
Bills and Papers	Irregular	No	Listed in and therefore indexed in the *Journal*
Journal	Sessional	Sessional index (in the volume) Decennial index (separate volume)	

The Printed Paper Office and the Distribution of Papers

The Printed Paper Office of the House of Lords services members of the House of Lords much as the Vote Office services members of the House of Commons, by supplying them with the published documents they need for their Parliamentary duties. A specialized department within the Parliament Office of the House of Lords has existed for this purpose since 1829 but a Clerk of Printed Papers only since the mid-nineteenth century.

The Printed Paper Office, conveniently situated near the Chamber, today works according to the terms set out in the 4th Report of the House of Lords Offices Committee of Session 1966–7, issuing peers with all Parliamentary documents and Command Papers, and non-Parliamentary material published by HMSO where they are referred to in a particular motion. If they have spoken in a debate peers may have six free copies of the relevant *Hansard*. Where they need extra copies of papers they may order these through the Printed Paper Office. The House of Lords has no Sale Office, but HMSO will then send peers copies of the Papers ordered, duly invoiced.

The holdings of the Printed Paper Office are more extensive than the Vote Office, with many papers being kept for five sessions plus the current session, rather than one session plus the current one, and with some sets of papers such as Acts and Command Papers the runs go much further back. The most important papers of the European Communities are also held for five years.

Although the Printed Paper Office's holdings of Parliamentary papers are more extensive than those of the Vote Office, there is no early morning distribution of papers such as is undertaken by the staff of the Deliverer of the Vote. The Office provides a daily list of papers laid before the House which is included in the Minutes of the House of Lords, a weekly list of Command Papers, Bills and Amendments, a weekly list of EEC publications identical to one produced by the Vote Office and a fortnightly list of Statutory Instruments laid before the House. With the aid of those lists and with the reference service of the House of Lords Library to back it up, the staff of the Printed Paper Office are able to keep on top of the growing quantity of publications, especially Parliamentary and EEC publications.

With regard to other publications, fact sheets, statistical information, etc., the Printed Paper Office interprets its role of supplying peers with publications more widely than the Vote Office interprets its role vis-à-vis Members of Parliament and it holds a lot of government and occasionally other printed material that the Vote Office would not expect to take. But then Members of the House of Commons have a much larger Library which takes all this material for its reference services and they more frequently make arrangements direct with Government Departments to receive such information on a regular basis.

The Library

The Library of the House of Lords was started in 1826 in an effort to bring some order into its mounting collection of records and books. Sir John Soane, who had been Clerk of the Works of the Palace for a generation and who was then building a library for the House of Commons in the Gothic style, was required to fit up a large Committee room which he was building, to be used as a Library

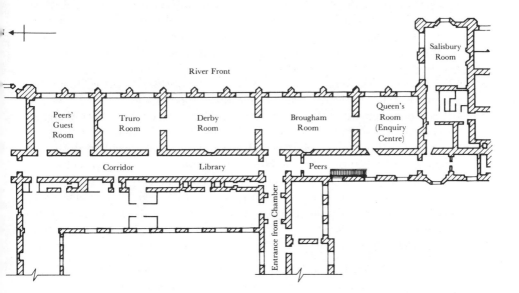

Layout of rooms in the Lords Library

for the Lords. He did so in a rich Renaissance style, making it look rather more comfortable than his Commons Library.[2]

Soane's Library was hardly damaged by the fire in 1834, and nearly all the materials were saved. Even before the fire Soane's Library was proving inadequate and a handsome present of some 1,700 books from the French Senate was proving an embarrassment. In 1834 a Committee called for an extra room to be added and this was completed in late 1837, and these buildings continued in use until 1851[3] when the Library was finally moved into its present handsome set of rooms along the terrace front and one floor up. In the overall planning of the new Palace of Westminster it balanced the House of Commons Library.

For over a hundred years the Library gradually grew, always strong in law, sometimes receiving interesting collections, and in 1908 Edmund Gosse produced an interesting author and subject catalogue with a brief history of the Library as an introduction and two appendices listing special collections.

In 1922 a Library Committee was formed – it is a Sub-committee of the Offices Committee – which in the words of a recent report 'did little and did it very well'. The Library is for Members of the House, Lords of Appeal and, of course, the officials.

In recent years two events have increased pressure on the Library. In the first place the Lord Chancellor's office has grown very considerably. Secondly, the creation under the Life Peerages Act 1958 of a large number of Life peers has resulted in a new clientele. On 4 May 1976 the Leader of the House appointed a Working Group to review the Library, the first comprehensive review since it was started just 150 years before. The Chairman was Viscount Eccles, then serving as the first Chairman of the Board of the British Library, and among the seven other members were several who, like Viscount Eccles, had been members of the House of Commons previously and who had used the more extensive services available there.

The report of the Working Group, which was to the Leader of the House and which was referred to the Offices Committee, appeared in March 1977[4] just before the retirement of the then Librarian. His successor, Mr Roger Morgan, had been on the staff of the House of Commons Library for many years, so there coincided in the summer of 1977 the possibility of new ideas and demands, rather as had taken place in the House of Commons a generation before.

The 33 recommendations in the report, although they may make quiet reading, do represent a radical change of outlook. When the report was debated[5] it became clear that the Library was to be rearranged to meet the need for up-to-date services. Among recommendations which recorded this spirit of change were the following:

1   The House of Lords Library should be organised to provide Peers ... with an information service more nearly comparable to that provided by the House of Commons.
8   An Enquiries Centre is essential to the work of the Library.
14   The majority of the legal volumes including Lord Truro's Collection (a handsome collection of old law material housed in the Library Truro Room) should be transferred to the Corridors near the Appellate Committees' Rooms.
30   A joint working-party drawn from the Library staff of the two Houses should be set up to discuss at regular intervals matters of common concern.
32   The Library should be linked as soon as possible to computer data bases carrying bibliographical and other information of use to Peers.
33   Peers should be asked to accept the necessity of microform.

Most significant of all was recommendation 5: 'The proposal for a complete merger between the House of Lords and the House of Commons Libraries should be rejected.'

Just as in the 1820s Soane had been required to build separate Libraries for each House really only a few yards apart, so in the 1970s the idea of a Parliamentary Library at Westminster was firmly rejected.

Since 1977 a great number of changes and a great deal of work has been achieved. First the staff has grown from ten, including two senior staff, in 1976, to 17, including four senior staff, by the end of 1978. The effect of this has been that in addition to the Librarian and Assistant Librarian there are now two Library Clerks to undertake research for peers. Although this does not give capacity for any real specialization it does mean that now fewer peers are using the House of Commons Library Research Division. (The number who used it was always small compared with Members of the Commons.) A number of Reference Sheets rather in the style of House of Commons Reference Sheets of a few years ago, i.e. strong on references, less so on comment or background, have been prepared. The second result of more staff has been the establishment of an Enquiry Centre in the Queen's Room and this now corresponds to the Oriel and Reference Rooms in the House of Commons Library. Here a Lord may find both current official papers and standard reference works. There is also now a booklending facility not only from the Library's own stock, which has always existed, but in recent years from outside libraries including a multiple subscription for recently published books from Harrods. The result of this has been that those peers who used to use the House of Commons facilities in this respect no longer do so. A third result of this increase in staff has been progress in the re-cataloguing of the Library. Pre-1950 holdings are being recatalogued onto cards and by early 1979 when the procedures had been well established, progress was running at well over 1000 items a year. The Library will be sending records for its quite extensive collection of eighteenth century material to the British Library's Short Title Catalogue in course of preparation. References for earlier materials will be sent to the Pollard and Redgrave or Wing Short Title Catalogue as appropriate. Post-1950 holdings are being catalogued in an entirely different way. The House of Lords Library has joined the LOCAS system established by the British Library for cataloguing its current intake and recataloguing its post-1950 imprints. After selecting records by ISBN or Dewey number, editing them and adding a library location or creating a new record for items not in the British Library data, the records are sent to the British Library from which a catalogue on microfiche in three sequences (namely, author and title, by Dewey classification and by Library of Congress subject headings) and a computer printed PRECIS index come back monthly. Except for law, Parliament and one or two other groups of material post-1950 imprints are being arranged on the shelves in broad Dewey order. One result of this system is that the House of Lords Library is able to give copies of its microfiche catalogue to the Library of the House of Commons and the House of Lords Record Office.

The BLAISE terminal in the Library is used for external databases via the telephone network and several of these have been signed up including IRS (Information Retrieval Service) via Euronet, Lockheed Dialog, Orbit and the Information Bank provided by the *New York Times*, together with those which are part of the BLAISE service. The Library has, like the House of Commons Library, access via VDUs to the four House of Lords databases, including that of the House of Lords Library itself. This consists of over 5,000 documents covering the Library's intake of House of Lords Departmental, Stationery Office and Commons papers, Bow Group, CBI, OECD, PSI publications and some UN and other material from intergovernmental organizations.

The Working Party on the Library had been aware of the usefulness of the press-cuttings service of the House of Commons Library and in the autumn of 1978 an arrangement was made for the House of Commons Library's cuttings before they were filed to be microfiched by the House of Lords Library. To date, this co-operation has worked very well. One further aspect of the introduction of modern technology into the House of Lords Library must be mentioned. At the end of 1978 the Library took delivery of one of the first television sets equipped to receive the Post Office's PRESTEL system, to which the Information Office of both the House of Commons Library and the House of Lords contribute, so that peers were very early confronted with this new source of information.

In terms of size of staff it might be argued that the House of Lords Library, following the seminal Report of the Working Party, has now reached a stage of development not unlike the House of Commons Library at the end of the 1940s.

The suite of rooms forming the House of Lords Library, looking over the Thames, and from the Salisbury Room down the river to the City, is only a little smaller in size than the Commons Library and the accommodation has to be shared by peers with fewer staff. This is important because fewer peers than Members now have rooms so that the Library can be very full at times. It has a mellow, comfortable air with its background of red-leather chairs, dark wood and more than a sprinkling of leather bindings. The Library is very strong on law as you would expect with its particular responsibility to the Appellate Committee of the House of Lords. In 1978 this sat for 130 days, hearing 41 cases and required 13,000 volumes from the Library together with many photocopies of material. Two members of the Library staff are especially involved in this work. There is also the service that they provide, as a matter of courtesy, for the Department of the Lord Chancellor. The legally qualified staff in this Department rose from 13 in 1965 to 26 in 1977 and as it has no law library of its own, its use of the House of Lords Library has naturally grown. But the House of Lords Library is much more than a legal collection. Like the House of Commons Library it has many of the standard historical and topographical works because many of the Librarians of the House of Lords have been bookmen, such as Edmund Gosse 1904-14, Sir Charles Clay 1922-56, and recently Christopher Dobson 1956-77.

The House of Lords Library has two special collections which bring real distinction to it as a scholarly Library. The first of these is the working library of some two thousand law books, a gift of the widow of Lord Chancellor Truro (1782-1855). The second is the two thousand tracts which belonged to the third Sir Robert Peel and which were purchased in 1897.

The Truro library includes a large series of legal notebooks of the eighteenth and nineteenth centuries, including those of the Hon. Henry Bathurst. The collection of Peel Tracts was started when Sir Robert Peel was Chief Secretary of Ireland 1812-16. This Library was selected by William Shaw Mason who published a catalogue as *Bibliotheca Hibernica* in Dublin in 1823. Mostly of Irish interest the collection ran to 170 volumes and really came to an end at the Union in 1800. Subsequently the Peel Tracts were continued through the first half of the nineteenth century especially by the third Sir Robert Peel and the collection which was purchased in 1897, listed in 1908, and remains in the Library, runs to some 300 volumes covering mostly Irish history from the late seventeenth century to the first half of the nineteenth century.

If any Lord travelled up to Westminster to visit his Library for the first time for, say, four years he would be astonished by the changes that would strike him. The last time he was there the Queen's Room was a museum housing some of the more dramatic documents from the House of Lords Record Office which hushed guests might be shown if the House were not sitting. Today it has telephones, microfilm reader/printers, two computer terminals, and a large television set showing PRESTEL information. If he wanted research done, he would probably have gone down the long corridor to the House of Commons Library. Today he will discuss it and probably have it carried out by House of Lords staff. (The new House of Lords library staff had an induction course in the House of Commons Library and use its extensive facilities quite regularly.) A generation of change in a few years. But at the same time the Working Party had stipulated that modernization should be 'not at the expense of the atmosphere characteristic of the Lords Library'[6] and our visiting peer would find that although many of the volumes had been rearranged, including the removal from the Library suite of the distinguished Truro Library, he could quickly settle back into traditional surroundings.

What of the future? Now that a clear decision has been taken not to propose the amalgamation of the Library of the House of Commons and the House of Lords, the Lords Library's role will be closely linked to the future of the House of Lords itself. That has been a debated question for years. And as with services at the House of Commons end of the Palace of Westminster, one fundamental constraint on the Library's development is the limited accommodation available so that a large staff, even if desired, would cause serious problems. However, in the 1980s with the aid of modern technology it is certainly possible to get more work done by the same number of people than, let us say, in the 1950s. For this reason the House of Lords Library is taking advantage of all the possibilities offered by these new techniques. It is likely that any further expansion will result from the needs of Lords for further research.

There is, however, one new element in the situation and that is the computer. For centuries the House of Commons and the House of Lords have been two very distinct institutions, whether it is a matter of role or custom, publishing policy or Library, but the advent of new and very expensive technology is bound to lead to reorientation. When, at the end of 1978, it was decided to appoint a Computer Development Officer for Parliament, although he was placed on the establishment of the Administration Department of the House of Commons, he was made – the first person ever apart from the Private Bill Examiner – a senior offical of the House of Commons and the House of Lords. There could not be a clearer pointer to the way in which the introduction of computers makes institutions re-examine their relationships and methods.

BIBLIOGRAPHY OF OFFICIAL REPORTS AND LIST OF PRINTED CATALOGUES

Report by the Lords Committees in 1825 appointed to view the Parliament Office etc.   1825   HL (206) CXCII p.747

Report by the Lords Committees in   1826-7   HL (58) CCXIX p.505
   1826 appointed to view the Parliament Office etc .. Library
Further Account of Proceedings ... Library 1826-7   HL (45) CCXX p.25
Report from the Select Committee appointed in
   1827:   1826-7   HL (82) CCXIX p.499
   re-appointed in 1828   1828   HL (181) CCXXXVII p.331
   re-appointed in 1829   1829   HL (105) CCXLIV p.351
Report from the Select Committee respecting 1834   HL (20) XXI p.587
   Additions to the Library of the House
First Report from the Select Committee   1856   HL (71) XXIV p.261
   relative to the Library
Library Sub-Committee of the Offices Committee
1922:   Annual Report from the Library Sub-Committee to the offices
   Committee. Noted in the House of Lords *Journal* but not printed *in
   extenso*. A fuller version is in the Minutes of the Offices Committee
   which are not printed.

The Library of the House of Lords: a short guide 1972

The Library of the House of Lords: a short history 1972

Report of the Working Group on the Library of the House of Lords
                                        1976-7   HL (84)
House of Lords *Library Bulletin* 1978 - Irregular.

Printed Catalogues
Catalogue of the Library of the House of Lords (exclusive of the Legal Section) by
Edmund Gosse. 2 Vols, 1908. Volume 1 is an author catalogue and volume 2 is a
catalogue of special collections and a list of the Peel Tracts.

Notes

1 Figures are taken from the House of Lords Weekly Information Bulletin of
  14 June 1980.
2 Soane, J. *Designs for public and private buildings*. 1828. Plate 28 illustrates both
  'new' libraries.
3 *History of the King's Works*. Vol. VI 1973. 525.
4 *The Library of the House of Lords: Report of the Working Group* 1976-7 HL(84).
5 HL Deb. Vol.389 cols 209-28.
6 1976-7 HL(84). 4.

CHAPTER THREE

Parliament

Statutes and Statutory Instruments

STATUTES

When a Public Bill has been through all its stages and is given the Royal Assent in the House of Lords it is promulgated and published by HMSO as an Act of Parliament receiving an arabic chapter number. This numbering starts afresh each calendar year. The text of the Act is divided into Sections and if it changes existing statute law, then the Acts changed are listed in a schedule. The date of coming into force is either stated in the Act, or it gives power to a Minister to lay a Statutory Instrument(s) before Parliament, indicating when it will become law.

At the end of the year, all the Public General Acts and the General Synod Measures are brought out in a set of bound volumes with a combined title and subject index in all the volumes. In addition there is a Chronological Table showing how previous Acts were affected by legislation passed during the year.

Every year there is a further publication, *Annotations to Acts*, which contains amendments to previous legislation caused by the passing of Public General Acts during the year. This work, the publication of which is getting seriously in arrears, is arranged chronologically by the Act which has to be amended and a few libraries make these amendments to keep up to date the text of their Statutes Revised 3rd edition 1948 and their Public General Acts since 1949.

Periodically the statutes have been republished amended up to date. The last time this was done was in the third edition of the Statutes Revised of 1950 bringing the statute law up to date as at the end of 1948 but no further revised editions in this form are planned.

The *Index to the Statutes* published most years is a comprehensive alphabetical subject index in two volumes. The latest edition in two volumes covers the Statutes 1235–1976. A companion volume, *Chronological Table of the Statutes*, currently covers the period 1235–1978 in two volumes and lists by session until the end of 1962, by calendar year from 1963 onwards, all statutes arranged by their chapter numbers. It indicates their status at the time of going to press and is the correct source to trace the history of an Act.

In recent years however publication of the *Statutes in Force* has started. This is a loose-leaf subject arrangement of updated statutes, and so far about fifty five volumes have been published covering among other subjects agency, agriculture, bankruptcy, elections, immigration, income and corporation tax, property, road traffic, sale of goods, town and country planning, and weights and measures. New volumes are being added quite rapidly; they are updated with loose-leaf amendments at least once a year and where there is a major amending Act this is brought out more quickly still. Increasingly they are becoming the most up to date authoritative text of the statute law although keeping them up to date does involve quite a lot of routine work.

So far only Public General Acts have been discussed but we now turn to Local and Personal Acts. These also are brought out individually with a particular chapter number, this time a roman number. Order Confirmation Acts are also in this series. HMSO publish a list of the Acts together with a detailed subject index for each calendar year. There is a general index which covers a period 1801–1947 and a supplementary volume 1948–66. The individual Acts are, of course, listed in *Government Publications.*

The making of statutes, both Public General Acts and Local and Personal Acts, is a vital part of Parliament's work and also of its dialogue with electors. There is also, however, delegated legislation, now called Statutory Instruments (formerly Statutory Rules and Orders), which also impinge on Parliament's work and, of course, on electors.

STATUTORY INSTRUMENTS

Statutory Instruments are prepared by government Departments in order to carry out the detailed administration that the Government of the day requires. They are important because they have the force of statute law. Many of them are issued under a Public General Act which Parliament has already passed. There are over 2000 a year of these Statutory Instruments and Parliament examines over half of them. Most of those examined have been laid before Parliament for information and to enable Parliament before they come into effect to comment on them and even to get them withdrawn if it is considered that there are grounds for doing so. The procedure covers many aspects of Parliament's work, in miniature.

First, the Statutory Instruments which are laid before the House appear listed in the annex to the Votes and Proceedings and later in the *Journal.* They are then set either before the Joint Select Committee on Statutory Instruments (i.e. Members of both House of Commons and House of Lords meeting jointly) or the House of Commons Select Committee where surveillance is limited to the House of Commons. The Select Committee examines them to check that this subordinate legislation is within the particular powers which Parliament has delegated to the Executive by the 'parent Act' and decides which instruments it wants further information on, asking first for a written memorandum and, if still not satisfied, then oral evidence from civil servants from the responsible Department. Finally, if it is still not satisfied that the Statutory Instrument is in order, it draws the attention of the House to it in a Report to the House. If it does this then it publishes evidence in its Report. The Statutory Instrument should then be debated in the House of Commons or, if there is not time, in a special Standing Committee.

Statutory Instruments, initially published individually, are given an arabic number starting at the beginning of each calendar year and should be cited by the year followed by the number, e.g, SI 1978/1111. They are listed together in the Stationery Office Daily List, and have their own separate publication, 'List of Statutory Instruments registered in the month of', the index to which cumulates twice a year. The Statutory Instruments are republished in volume form at the end of the year. This annual republication runs to several volumes arranged numerically, i.e. chronologically. It includes a classified list of local instruments and a table of effects of the year's Statutory Instruments on both Statutes and Statutory Instruments. There is also a numerical list of public Statutory Instruments.

Every two years there is published the *Index to Government Orders* which is a subject index to the Statutory Instruments and Orders in force which corresponds to the *Index to the Statutes*. In alternative years there is published the *Supplement to Index to Government Orders*, to keep it up-to-date. There is also an accompanying annual volume *Table of Government Orders* which is a list of general instruments arranged chronologically from 1671 – with an indication as to whether they have been revised, repealed, etc. This corresponds to the *Chronological Table of the Statutes* and is updated half-yearly with a *Table of Government Orders Noter-up.*

European Community Affairs

On 1 January 1973 Parliament became involved in a whole new network of information. It was then that we became members of the European Communities. The House of Commons Library had, since the start of the original three European Communities, taken their documents in French, and also those few which for convenience were made available in English, but from 1 July 1973 all the documentation started to appear in a new official language – English.

Parliament was bound to become entangled in the work of the Communities, not least because of the importance of law in European Community thinking and administration and throughout the debate in the House of Commons on the European Communities Bill, Members continually showed their concern for the powers of Parliament in the forthcoming situation and the manner in which they were going to be informed by the Government on Community matters.[1] But joining the Communities was like marriage; there really was no halfway house and the Westminster Parliament's power in certain areas was truncated. What was set up, therefore, after we joined the Communities, was a system of surveillance by Parliament and a routine of the Government reporting Community developments to Parliament.

The main institutions of the European Communities are the Commission, the executive arm, the 13 Commissioners each with certain 'subject areas' under their control and some ten thousand civil servants; the Council, which consists of a Minister from the nine member countries and where work is supported by the Committee of Permanent Representatives; the European Parliament, which consists of 410 Members who since 1979 have been directly elected and the Court of Justice, the final arbiter on legal matters, which has nine judges, one from each Member country. The Commission and the Council are situated in Brussels, the Parliament and the Court are in Luxembourg.[2]

The 'constitution' of the Community institutions is the original Treaty of Rome and various other accession treaties including the one which took the UK into the Communities. These are seldom amended but major constitutional changes do require domestic legislation – witness the recent European Assembly Elections Act. The EC secondary legislation is designed to maintain and indeed develop the implications of the original Treaties or primary legislation and it is the job of the Commission to initiate such legislation, in the form of proposals for Regulations and Directives.

Before turning to the question of Community legislation, mention must be made of the Government's promised method of keeping Parliament informed on Community matters in general. Ministers regularly tell the two Houses, as accurately as they can, of the proposed agenda of future Council meetings and when they have attended them, they report back with a statement in Parliament. Secondly, the Government publishes a six-monthly report on developments in the Community and this is regularly debated. Thirdly, Parliamentary Questions on Community matters have a specially reserved place in the rota of Questions. Fourthly, the Prime Minister reports back to the House of Commons after European Council or 'summit' conferences. In addition, the House of Commons and the House of Lords set aside up to four other days in the session to debate Community affairs. Finally, like the draft legislative proposals from the Commission, the budget of the Communities is referred to the relevant Select Committees of the House of Commons and House of Lords.

In small matters the Commission has power to issue Regulations and Directives on its own, but on larger matters many institutions get involved, including both the House of Commons and the House of Lords. Briefly, the procedure is as follows.

The Commission, after consultation with national governments, pressure groups etc., produces a draft Regulation or Directive and sends it to the Council, as a proposal, via the Committee of Permanent Representatives. At this point most of the proposals are referred to the European Parliament, which is a consultative organization not a legislature, to the Economic and Social Committee which is also a consultative organization and, in the case of the UK, to the Cabinet Office. The Cabinet Office sends copies of the proposal to the Department reponsible for the subject and to the House of Commons and the House of Lords. The draft is, in time, published in the *Offical Journal of the European Communities* in the 'C' series. What lies behind the procedures? The Commission, which alone has the powers of initiative, has sent proposals to the

Council, which alone has the powers of legislating. On the way, the European Parliament and often the Economic and Social Committee have been consulted and national parliaments too have a chance to scrutinize the proposals. This is to inform Members of national parliaments and to enable them, if they think it appropriate, to bring pressure to bear on the Minister who will be a member of the Council which legislates. In this way, the UK represented voice is heard and Ministers remain responsible to Parliament, a cardinal point of the Parliamentary system.

In July 1973 both the House of Commons and the House of Lords set up Select Committees to examine how each House could respond to this new situation. It created both a new constitutional problem and a new information problem. Both of them came up with the idea of a Select Committee which would examine the legislative proposals and refer certain of them to the House for debate. The House of Lords, however, decided on a more elaborate structure of Committees and to devote more time to the problem.

The House of Commons Select Committee on European Legislation was set up following a statement in the House of Commons on 2 May 1974. The Committee consists of 16 Members from all parties and they normally receive a copy of a draft Regulation two or three days after it becomes available in Brussels. They are required to report to the House on the legal and political importance of the draft Regulation and to recommend whether the House should consider it further. To help them, the Department in whose remit the subject of the draft regulations comes, is required to submit an explanatory memorandum, signed by the Minister, normally within two weeks of the arrival of the draft. This written assessment may be followed up by civil servants being required to give further oral or written evidence. While this is going on, there are four House of Commons staff who are preparing internal briefs on the draft for the Committee. Finally a special legal adviser, also on the House of Commons staff, aids the Committee. This filter process results in a report to the House listing those proposals which the Committee consider the House should examine further.

The debate that follows the Committee's report is on a motion: 'That this House takes note of Commission numbers ...', and lasts an hour and a half. The main point of the debate is to arrive at a view about the particular proposal and in practice a vote on the motion is seldom taken. It is the chance for the elected representatives to inform the Minister of their views on the proposal before he goes to 'legislate' in the Council. Because of a lack of time to debate the Commission documents, Standing Committees have occasionally been used for less important proposals.

The House of Lords has a more elaborate and probably more effective way of working. Up to 90 Members of the House of Lords may be involved in this work. The first sift of documents is made by the Chairman of the Select Committee on the European Communities and about a third are passed on for Committee scrutiny. There are six subject sub-committees covering finance, economics and regional policy; trade and treaties; health, employment, education and social

affairs; food and agriculture; energy, transport and research; and environment, and each tackles proposals which are relevant. A further law sub-
committee, with a legal adviser, examines the legal implications of all
proposals. As with the Commons Committee the Lords Committee on the
European Communities receives the explanatory memorandum from the
government Department and may take further oral and written evidence.
When the main Committee make their report to the House of Lords on
proposals that should be debated it is sometimes an elaborate one, giving the
background of the proposal and their views.

To complete this period of scrutiny, the European Parliament will have
assigned the draft proposal to one of its specialist Committees which will report
back to the Parliament as a whole, and similarly the Economic and Social
Committee will have considered the draft legislation. These two European
bodies report their views to the Council direct and finally the Ministers in the
council take the decision to legislate and promulgate it through the 'L' Series of
the *Official Journal of the European Communities.*

Obviously this is rather a simplified account of the new role for Parliament
that membership of the European Communities has brought. Let us now look
at the documentation involved.

1   Draft Regulations and Directives are not published documents, though it is
     possible to get copies from the European Communities Information Office
     in London. They are published in time in the 'C' Series of the *Official
     Journal.*
2   The explanatory memorandum prepared in the government Departments
     for the Select Committees of both Houses are not published.
3   The briefs for the Select Committees prepared by staff in the Clerk's
     Department of the House of Commons are not published.
4   The oral and written evidence taken by the Select Committees is sometimes
     published in the Sessional Papers.
5   The Reports by Select Committees to both Houses are published as
     Sessional Papers of either the House of Commons or the House of Lords.
     The House of Lords reports its sifting work regularly in its Fortnightly
     Report Series and individually on draft proposals it considers important.
     The House of Commons reports briefly on all draft proposals indicating
     those it thinks should be debated.
6   Debates on the legislation in both Houses or in Standing Committees are
     published as Parliamentary or Standing Committee Debates.
7   The European Parliament Committee which examines the draft proposal
     reports to the European Parliament through a European Parliament
     Working Document. The Debate, in the plenary session of the European
     Parliament, on the resolution, will appear in the *Official Journal Annex.* The
     resolution on the report appears in the European Parliament minutes. The
     Economic and Social Committee opinion on the draft proposals is
     published in the C Series of the *Official Journal.*

8   The Council promulgates its legislation in the L Series of the *Official Journal*.

Note: Draft Instruments may be known either by the Com. number assigned by the Commission or by a four-digit number followed by the year (e.g. 4669/79), assigned to the document by the Council in Brussels. The latter is adopted by government bodies in the UK, and will be used for all *Hansard* and other UK official references. The instrument will continue to be identified in official EEC documents only by its Com. number. Until the end of 1978 these Council Numbers were prefixed by the letters R or S.

The Government's regular six-monthly Reports to Parliament on developments in the European Communities is published as a Command Paper. In addition to a subject by subject report, there is a very useful annex listing all the meetings which have taken place both of the European Council, i.e. 'summit' meetings and those of the Council of Ministers. It includes the dates of the meetings and the name of the Minister attending.

These Reports are generally debated on the Motion to 'take note of the Report...' which is a regular chance to debate Community matters. These debates, together with the Government's regular statement about future business to be taken by the Council of Ministers of the European Communities, appear in the Parliamentary Debates. Finally, Parliamentary Questions and Answers on Community matters together with up to four further days for debate each year are also to be found in the Parliamentary Debates.

Although Parliament has lost certain powers subsequent to our joining the European Communities it has nevertheless developed into an important source of information. It remains to be seen how things alter now the European Parliament is directly elected as there are no longer the 36 Members of the European Parliament who were also Members of either one or other of the Houses at Westminster and who were an important informal source of information for Parliament on European Community matters. At the time of writing there are no plans for any modification of Parliament's procedures as a result of the changes in the composition of the European Parliament.

Parliamentary Records from the Past

Although Parliament itself commemorated its seven hundredth anniversary in 1965, it will not be until 1997 that the five hundredth anniversary of the beginning of the accumulation of records within Parliament will arise. It was only in 1497 that the then Clerk of the Parliaments decided to keep the original Acts of Parliament of the session, instead of passing them over to Chancery as had been done previously, because early Clerks of the Parliament came from Chancery. To this day it is the Clerk of the Parliaments who is responsible for the records of Parliament. Therefore if you wish to consult Parliamentary materials prior to 1497 you must look for them in the Chancery records in the Public Record Office, not in the Parliamentary Records at Westminster.

Slowly, at first, these records built up under the Clerk of the Parliaments but during the Tudor period a rather casual attitude was sometimes adopted and certain records were lost.

In the early seventeenth century two energetic Clerks of the Parliaments, Robert Bowyer (1609–21) and Henry Elsynge (1621–35), took the records in hand and the collection was well organized and stored in the Jewel Tower still standing opposite the Palace of Westminister. There they remained for centuries, fortunately for historians, as they were beyond the reach of the fire in 1834. When after the fire Barry planned the new Palace of Westminister, he included what was then the largest square tower in the world, the Victoria Tower, specifically to house the collection of Parliamentary Records. In 1864 they were moved back across the road from the Jewel Tower to the Victoria Tower and there they have remained ever since.

The records of the House of Commons itself started to be collected during the Tudor period but as with the Parliamentary Records it was only during the early seventeenth century that they became properly organized. This collection, however, was kept in the Palace of Westminster itself so that when the great fire in 1834 reduced nearly all the old palace to ashes, they were nearly all destroyed with the fortunate exception of the manuscript journals. The loss was a severe one as in 1834 Bill papers existed from 1558, Petitions from 1607 and Returns of information required by the House from 1642. The loss of the originals of these series is partly offset by the fact that some of the more important of them had been ordered to be printed and have survived as 'separates' or have been entered in the *Journal* itself. But despite the tenacity of scholars in tracing printed examples of the papers or indeed manuscript copies of some of them to fill the gaps, especially for the period 1715–1800, the loss caused by the fire was grave.

There are four main groups of documents among the Parliamentary Records. First, there is the large collection of House of Lords papers which, as mentioned, survived the fire. Second, there is the much smaller collection of House of Commons documents which survived the fire. Since 1834 both these collections are largely complete. Third, there are the collections of documents from other offices at Westminster and, finally, both Houses have certain historical collections, though again those of the House of Lords are by far the greater.

The first of these groups is that of the Clerk of the Parliaments dating from 1497 and the most important record here is the original Acts of Parliament. Until 1849 these were engrossed on vellum rolls. They look like 'books' in classical times but since 1849 they have been printed on vellum in codex form. These are the authoritative text of the statutes of the land and since 1849 each one has been signed by the Clerk of the Parliaments or his Deputy. The Public Acts have been published since 1483 but before 1800 Private Acts were frequently not printed which is why the Index to Personal and Local Acts only starts from that date.

The manuscript Journals of the House of Lords are really the next most important record of the Clerks of the Parliaments. They date from 1510. Then there are the Sessional Papers of the House of Lords, firstly those connected with Bills. These include material such as Petitions, Amendments, Proceedings in Committees, Deposited Plans (from 1794) and other evidence concerning Private Bills from 1572, and certain similar documents for Public Bills from 1558. The collection of House of Lords Committee Proceedings dates from 1610, the period when the Parliamentary Records were being organized by Robert Bowyer.

Turning from the proceedings of the House of Lords on legislation to other papers, we have Petitions from 1531 including those from private groups and individuals and from 1621 the Judicial Records of the House of Lords when it is working in that special capacity.

Published calendars of this huge collection of House of Lords sessional papers covering 1450–1678 are in the Appendices of the first nine Reports of the Historical Manuscripts Commission and the documents from 1678–1692, often calendared *in extenso*, are in the Appendices to the 11th–14th Reports. The period 1693–1718 is in the series of twelve volumes 'the Calendar of the Manuscripts of the House of Lords'. Although the earlier of these volumes have been reprinted it is unlikely that the series will be continued (for details see pp. 114–15).

The second group of documents, those of the House of Commons, consists firstly of the manuscript journals from 1547 with serious gaps during the reign of Elizabeth I. There are 241 volumes covering the period 1547–1800. As with the House of Lords Journal these were first printed during the eighteenth century. There are also a few House of Commons papers for the period 1603–89 which survived the fire and which are included among the House of Lords Sessional papers. All the other House of Commons papers were destroyed.

So far we have been describing the manuscript collections of the House of Lords and the House of Commons before 1834. The Parliamentary Records, however, also include fine collections of the printed Minutes of the House of Lords from when they started in 1835 and the printed Votes and Proceedings of the House of Commons from when they started in 1680.

Since 1834 the collections of manuscripts and printed documents of the two Houses are largely complete.

The third group of Parliamentary Records are those which have come from various offices and officials of Parliament. Included here are a small number of records from Black Rod's Office and a large collection of the records of the Lord Great Chamberlain. From the House of Commons there is a collection of records of the Serjeant at Arms and also of the Fees Office.

The fourth and final group of documents, both manuscript and printed, which form the Parliamentary Records, goes under the broad title Historical Collections. There are two groups of these, those of the House of Lords Record Office, and those of the House of Commons Library. Included among the House of Lords Collections are the Braye Manuscripts 1572–1731 which includes papers of John Browne, Clerk of the Parliaments 1638–49 and 1660–91. There are also photocopies of the Electoral Reform Society Records 1884-1949 and a collection of photographs of the fabric of the Palace of Westminster made in 1905. There are the papers of the Hansard family 1842-90, including the accounts of the printing firm and also the papers of Sir J. G. Shaw-Lefevre, who was Clerk of the Parliaments 1855-75. The Historical Collections of the House of Commons Library are less extensive but they include the Brand papers 1855-96. Henry Brand was Speaker 1872-84. Other nineteenth-century collections include the notebooks of Sir Thomas Erskine May 1834-6 and 1857-82 who was assistant librarian of the House of Commons, but who is better known as a Clerk of the House and the originator of *May's Parliamentary Practice* which reached a nineteenth edition in 1976.

This random comment on the collection of Parliamentary Records – there are over three million of them – is designed to indicate the range of this great public collection. There is an admirable work *Guide to the Records of Parliament* by Maurice Bond which apart from fulfilling its title gives a great deal of other detail on the working of Parliament over the centuries.

In a sense this great collection is the end of the story of 'Parliament and Information'. The hundreds of thousands of documents which have been submitted to or written by Parliament over nearly five centuries, if they survived the 1834 fire, still rest only a stone's throw from the two Chambers where the national debate continues. Included are some moving documents, among them the Death Warrant for the execution of Charles I with the Parliamentarian Oliver Cromwell's signature third down on the left-hand side; some touching letters between Charles I and his wife Henrietta Maria; the Royal Commission and Act of Attainder which led to the execution of young Katharine Howard in 1542; the House of Commons Journal of 1621 from which a furious King James I tore out an offending Protestation, and the Petition of Right which his son had finally to accept in 1628 with the note '*Soit droit fait come est desiré*' written by the Clerk of the Parliaments, that same Henry Elsynge who was busy tidying up the collections of records at the time. There are neat reports on the Navy by the arch-bureaucrat and diarist Samuel Pepys and the less neatly written memorandum from Buckingham Palace by Sir Herbert Samuel when, on 24 August 1931, King George V brought Ramsay MacDonald and Baldwin together there to discuss the formation of a National Government and then tactfully withdrew. There is the Act of Union between Scotland and England with the English signatories on the left-hand side and the Scots on the right. There is a further Act of 1978 designed to give the Scots the chance to vote themselves a devolved Assembly in Edinburgh. Every decade, indeed every year of our history has contributed information to Parliament and thus sustained its work.

A Note on Computers

This note on the use of computers at Westminster is in two parts. The first part covers the fairly short history of the development of the use of computers and progress towards planning their use in Parliament, excluding the House of Commons Library. The second part is an outline of the much longer involvement that the House of Commons Library has had in the question of the application of computer techniques to its indexing methods.

In 1973 a demonstration was given in the Palace of Westminster of the possibilities of full text retrieval of statute law from a small section of the newly printed Statutes in Force. These statutes are computer typeset and HMSO made the tapes of the text available to IBM for a display of information retrieval. Members and Officials of both Houses of Parliament saw the display which was a success. The Clerk of the Parliaments requested a fuller follow-up experiment which took place in the House of Lords in the summer of 1974 and at the same time the Central Computer Agency briefly examined the possibilities of applying computers to the work of Parliament. They suggested, firstly, a full-scale feasibility study of the problem of identifying areas for the application of computers, which Parliament declined to accept, and, secondly, the setting up of a Joint Computer Study Group which Parliament accepted. The Study Group was to consist of a clerk from both Houses and the newly appointed Computer Applications Officer in the House of Commons Library.

In 1975 the House of Lords started an experiment in information retrieval with a database which it proposed itself, namely, the documentation of the European Communities. From the beginning the system was to be on-line and in time a visual display unit (VDU) was made available not only in the Printed Paper Office of the House of Lords but also in the Library and the Vote Office of the House of Commons. A VDU was added to the Library of the House of Lords and other offices there.

At first the House of Lords entered the titles of Community legislation from the 'L' series of the *Official Journal* from 1973, the date of the UK accession, and later the Working Documents of the European Parliament, the Consultative Documents of the Commission, the *Official Journal* 'C' series, the *Official Journal Annex*, i.e. the European Parliament Debates and the Commission's Draft proposals for legislation. These last five groups of material were entered from January 1975. The text in the computer is the title and contents page of the various documents. There is no system of indexing; you are searching on the full text of these titles and contents pages. The computer used was that of the GLC and the STAIRS/ATMS system was adopted.

A second stage of development was when the House of Lords European Office and then the House of Commons Library started to update this database of European Community affairs with references to papers and proceedings of their respective Houses, those which related to the Draft proposals for legislation. This means that there is now available on-line each stage of the legislative history of European Community draft proposals from the moment they have arrived in this country and have been distributed to Parliament by the Government to their final adoption and promulgation by the Council in the *Official Journal* 'L' series. By mid 1980 there were about 10 000 documents in this database.

The House of Lords has since extended its databank beyond the European Communities material. A further three databases have been added covering House of Lords Library intake, the titles of the Acts of Parliament database and the House of Lords Registry database. The Library database of over 5000 items covers a wide range selectively of the Library's current intake. These include House of Lords papers, Bow Group and CBI publications, OECD, PSI material, TUC, UN, World Health Organization publications and miscellaneous pamphlets. The long titles of Acts of Parliament so far cover 1850-60 and number well over 3000 documents. It is intended to add in 'formatted fields' data concerning all related and subsidiary documents; in addition the Lords are forming a Registry File of Parliamentary procedure, which is likely to prove of great value to the Information Offices of each House.

While this concrete work was being undertaken by the House of Lords, on 13 May 1976 an informal Joint Committee of the House of Lords and the House of Commons was set up: 'to consider and advise on the contribution that computer-based systems might make towards meeting the information and other requirements of both Houses'.

The informal Joint Committee reported to the Houses on 18 January 1977 and started with the following clarion call for modern technology to come to the aid of Parliament:

> The Committee is unanimous in its belief that the introduction of computer-based systems into both Houses is essential if Parliament is to fulfil its proper constitutional role *vis-à-vis* the executive. Government is extending its control over an increasingly wide, complex and technical range of activities and Parliament must have access to information of a correspondingly wide variety to enable it to evaluate government policies and legislation and to anticipate the needs of the future. The quantity of information needed to fulfil this role efficiently is enormous, and it will place a growing burden on Members of both Houses and the officials who serve them. The Committee consider that Parliament's information services will be seriously impaired unless computer techniques are introduced as a matter of urgency, and that the offices of both Houses will become increasingly ill-equipped to carry out their work unless they also are able to take advantage of contemporary technology.[3]

The Committee recommended that: 'a formal joint Committee of both Houses should be appointed in the session 1976-7 to study the needs of Members and officials and to make recommendations on computer developments.'

Parliament does not normally move quite as quickly as was recommended but early in the session 1977-8 a Computer Sub-committee was added to the House of Commons (Services) Committee. This Sub-committee took written evidence from various Departments of the House including the Library Department and oral evidence from, among others, senior staff of the Library. A similar Computer Sub-committee was set up under the House of Lords Offices Committee with virtually the same terms of reference. At a joint meeting, after taking evidence from the Central Computer Agency and reviewing papers from Departments of both their Houses, they commissioned a survey by a consultant who was to identify areas of Parliamentary work which should be examined with a view to establishing computer-based facilities to aid Parliament. This consultant's survey recommended the appointment of a Computer Development Officer, a proposal immediately accepted, and a more extended feasibility study. The post of Computer Development Officer for Parliament was filled and he has been attached to the Administration Department of the House of Commons. At the same time the Clerk of the Parliaments appointed him a member of the Lords Information Services. He reports to both Computer Sub-Committees and this will enable him to promote a unified computer programme for Parliament.

The history of the House of Commons Library plans to computerize its indexing methods is a long one, well over ten years, but the salient stages can be set down briefly.

In 1968 the library staff at Culham laboratory, responding to an account of the Library's work published in the *New Scientist,* offered to co-operate with the House of Commons Library in putting on a display of Selective Dissemination of Information for Members of Parliament and a group of selected outsiders. The database was to be references from the main House of Commons indexes, the period of time was to be two months in the autumn of 1968 and the references, which ran to over 450 a week, 4500 in all, were to be printed out under one of 36 subject headings. The project was a great success and it took only two to three days to bring out the elegantly printed lists of references. In time a full index to this project was printed.

There was neither staff nor finance to continue the project, but during 1969 the Library negotiated with the then Office of Scientific and Technical Information (OSTI) for support for a study of the application of computers to the indexing methods of the House of Commons Library. The House of Commons itself backed this idea and the study was undertaken by ASLIB during 1970 with the report coming out in early 1971. The ASLIB report, which was not published, recommended that the Library should use computer power for its extensive indexing but the costings, which appear so modest today, clearly troubled the House and the main proposal was not adopted. However, the Library was empowered to add a Computer Services Officer to its staff, the first computer trained official to join the staff of Parliament and by 1974 the person was in post.

Since then important progress has been made. First, the Library has cleared its own mind with regard to a development programme. Second, the Central Computer Agency has agreed to offer financial and technical support. Third, an Operational Requirement of the Library's need has been drafted and agreed with the Central Computer Agency. Fourth, a thesaurus has been prepared for use with the House of Commons Library indexes. This represents work within the Library Department and in addition in January 1978 the House of Commons resolved that 'the Librarian be authorised to proceed with the introduction of computer-based indexing in the Library as soon as possible.'[4]

At the time of writing, mid 1980, the Library is working closely with

SCICON, the firm finally awarded the competitive tender to supply a bureau service for the computer-based indexing system and the first phase of the database, House of Commons Parliamentary Questions, is being built up to start a working system in the autumn of 1980. The new Computer Development Officer has been associated with this choice as it is clearly important that the Library's computer project is kept in line with the development of a Parliamentary system as a whole. Indeed the Services Committee recommended in July 1978 that: 'the Library's operational requirement be amended to take into account the need for overall applicability of any package that is finally chosen'[5] and this was done.

Ten years is a long time for any such development to take place. Whereas in 1968 it can be said that the House of Commons Library was in the van of computer application for information retrieval, certainly among Parliamentary libraries, in 1980 it is in the rear. In the Congressional Research Service the use of VDUs by staff for the retrieval of references to information is a matter of routine. In the Bundestag and, more recently, the Assemblée Nationale it is also an accepted working system, in the first case linked to its publishing programme. It is only the fact that the present manual indexing systems, started twenty-five years ago, are so good that it has been possible to sustain the level of service in the face of increasing demand from Members, the growing Library staff and more recently the growing personal staff, not to mention the great increase in official papers to be processed. But all this increased activity has led to the dispersal of Members and staff (two of the five Sections in the Research Division have left the Palace of Westminster in the last few years) and the old system of a single set of visible strip indexes available at one point in the Library will not be adequate for the future. The next ten years should see a complete change of technology both in the Library and with regard to other aspects of Parliament's work.

There is one other factor which may affect the whole question of Parliament's use of computers. If a programme to apply computer typesetting to the Stationery Office's printing of Parliamentary papers is carried through, then this change itself may well affect information retrieval for Parliament as a whole. There is likely to be scope for the better indexing of Hansard, Select Committee reports etc., and possibly for the more speedy drafting of Bills, tabling of Parliamentary Questions, etc. But that is a matter for the 1980s.

Select Committees and Information

No account of Parliament and information, however brief, should leave out mention of Parliament's oldest and most well-tried method of obtaining information – the Select Committee enquiry.

Excluding its own domestic matters, the House of Lords has only one Select Committee working regularly, it is concerned with the European Communities, and House of Lords *ad hoc* Select Committees are very rare. For that reason, and because methods in the two Houses are very similar, I have focused this account on the House of Commons.

In recent years between 250 and 300 Members of the House of Commons have served on Select Committees each session. This covers some seventeen or eighteen main Select Committees and their sub-committees and represents the scale of work before the introduction of the new Departmental Select Committee system in the autumn of 1979. The new system is likely to increase this work.

Some of these Committees are rather domestic in interest, such as the Services Committee with its four sub-committees and those concerning Procedure, Privilege, Members' Interests, Sound Broadcasting etc. Some have a special remit of surveillance like the Public Accounts Committee, or the Committees on Statutory Instruments or European Legislation, or on the Parliamentary Commissioner for Administration. Finally there are the new Departmental Select Committees.

All Select Committees are staffed by Clerks from the Department of the Clerk and most have the power to appoint specialist advisers with technical knowledge either to supply information which is not readily available or to elucidate matters of complexity within the Committee's order of reference. At the time of writing consideration is also being given as to how the full time staff assisting committees can best be strengthened. Of course Select Committees or their individual members may also call on the Library staff to prepare information or advise them.

Select Committees work by obtaining written and oral evidence from witnesses on the subject which they are studying. They may also travel to examine installations, etc. This evidence, submitted to them, comes from the relevant government Department, outside experts, pressure groups and any others who can help them with their task. Most Select Committees sit in public when taking evidence, but they invariably deliberate and draw up their report in private. It is the Committee itself which in practice decides how much of the oral and written evidence it has received will be published. Increasingly, the oral evidence taken is being published day by day as a House of Commons paper, each day's evidence having its own roman subnumber after the main arabic number.

The Select Committee can be an effective method of Parliament obtaining information. A good example of that was illustrated in the work of the Procedure Committee itself. When taking evidence it obtained and published for the first time a 'Memorandum of Guidance for officials appearing before Select Committees'. This is the paper which civil servants acting as witnesses before Select Committees will have read before appearing before the Committee and by publishing it the Committee made it easier for everyone to understand the relationship between witness and Committee when evidence is being taken. A Committee is required to report back to the House of Commons and each session there are published several volumes of reports and evidence. These are all House of Commons papers and therefore 'Ordered by the House of Commons to be printed' and they can be of fundamental importance and great interest. In recent years the amount published has tended to increase. The next stage regarding the Committee's work is that there may be a debate in the House on the report and possibly a vote. However, the same Procedure Committee noted that in 1970-77 only 44 out of 83 Select Committee reports were debated and that half of these debates were on the 25 reports on House of Commons domestic subjects. This means that only 22 debates took place on the 58 reports on non-domestic subjects. The Procedure Committe pressed for more time to debate these Select Committee reports especially following the setting up of the new Departmental Committee structure.

On 25 June 1979 the House of Commons accepted a number of motions which replaced the rather uncoordinated system of specialist Committees which had grown up since the War and especially since the 'Crossman reforms' of the 1960s, by a group of fourteen Departmental Select Committees. The Committees which disappeared included the Expenditure Committee, which had replaced the Estimates Committee, the Nationalised Industries Committee – both of these were of long standing – and the Overseas Development, Race Relations and Immigration and the Science and Technology Committees. The pattern of fourteen Departmental Committees which was set up is far more comprehensive and systematic and may well represent a significant change in Parliament's powers of obtaining information. The Committees are as follows:

Table 3.1 Departmental Select Committees

Name of Committee	Principal Government Departments concerned	Maximum number of Members*
Agriculture	Ministry of Agriculture, Fisheries and Food	9
Defence	Ministry of Defence	11
Education, Science and Arts	Department of Education and Science	9
Employment	Department of Employment	9
Energy	Department of Energy	11
Environment	Department of the Environment	11
Foreign Affairs	Foreign and Commonwealth Office	11
Home Affairs	Home Office	11
Industry and Trade	Department of Industry, Department of Trade	11
Scottish Affairs	Scottish Office	13
Social Services	Department of Health and Social Security	9
Transport	Department of Transport	11
Treasury and Civil Service	Treasury, Civil Service Department, Board of Inland Revenue, Board of Customs and Excise	11
Welsh Affairs	Welsh Office	11

*The quorum of each committee is 3, except for Scottish Affairs where it is 5.

Because of the number of Select Committees the establishment of sub-committees is not greatly encouraged and only the Foreign Affairs, Home Affairs and Treasury Committees have such power at the moment.

The Committees are appointed '... to examine expenditure, administration and policy of the principal government departments ... and associated public bodies'[6] and during the debate it was reaffirmed that: 'the objective of the new Committee structure will be to strengthen the accountability of Ministers to the House for the discharge of their responsibilities'. There is no Northern Ireland Departmental Select Committee but each Committee may examine relevant Northern Ireland matters. Finally there is a formal Liaison Committee made up of a member from each Select Committee, normally the Chairman, to consider general matters relating to the work of all Select Committees.

It is too early to assess the importance of this new element in the Select Committee system, but it is already clear that the House of Commons will be taking and publishing much more evidence.

These reforms suggest that this traditional method of Parliament obtaining information will again become of greater importance – 'again' because throughout the nineteenth and early twentieth centuries when 'Whitehall' was far smaller and the House of Commons more dominant, the role of Select Committees was of far greater importance than it has been in recent years. An interesting example of this is the way in which while the 1849 Public Libraries Act followed a House of Commons Select Committee report, the 1964 Act on the same subject followed a departmental report.

It is probable that even among specialists too little use is made of this public information which Parliament secures for its own work and much of which it orders to be printed and makes available to us all.

Notes

1 A Select Committee report from each House (1972–3 HL 67 and 194, HC 143, 463 I & II) proposed to each 'House' the details of how the Government should execute its responsibilities.
2 The Parliament is based in Luxembourg and meets there and in Strasbourg but its Committees in Brussels and elsewhere.
3 *Report of the Informal Joint Committee on Computers to the Leaders of both Houses.* 1976–7 HC78. 1.
4 *Fifth Report from the Select Committee on House of Commons (Services) Computer-based indexing for the Library.* 1976–7. HC377, xii.
5 *Seventh Report from the Select Committee on House of Commons (Services) Computer applications for the House of Commons.* 1977–8. HC617–1, p.ix.
6 House of Commons Standing Order No. 86A, para. 1.

PART II
Information from Parliament

CHAPTER FOUR

House of Commons

The Library's Public Information Office

In early 1977 the Accommodation and Administration Sub-Committee of the Services Committee began to take evidence from outside witnesses and officials of the House on the broad subject of services for the public. 'Your Committee', they reported, 'believe that there is a need for the House to ensure that the public is well informed about its work'.[1] They took evidence from the Principal Clerk, Information Services of the House of Lords (which had rearranged its information services three years previously and which had then created an Information Office for the public to learn about House of Lords matters) and from the Librarian of the House of Commons.

The upshot was a series of proposals made in a report of July 1977 which were subsequently authorized and most of which affect the Library Department. The most important of these was the creation of an Information Office 'for dealing initially with enquiries from the public'.

The Library, not surprisingly, has always dealt with the majority of enquiries from outside, and when a Branch Library was opened in the Norman Shaw (North) building in the summer of 1975 this work was moved there. Three years later this responsibility was recognized and other Departments of the House were encouraged to pass the enquiries which they received from outside the House to the Information Office. The Branch Library was already well equipped to help Members and their personal staff, so attaching this new Information Office responsibility to an ongoing service was rightly seen to be the most efficient way of offering this new public information service. In the first few months after the Information Office was opened in July 1978 the result was a doubling of enquiries from the public (as estimated by the Librarian when giving evidence) and, it is hoped, a reduction in the number of enquiries to other Departments of the House. The focus of the work is naturally information on the House of Commons, its history, membership and business, but enquiries do sometimes stray further than this. Two years after it opened the Office was answering nearly 50 000 enquiries a year and of these 44 per cent are from outside individuals and 35 per cent from outside organizations.

A second suggestion from the Services Committee was that the Information Office should prepare a *Weekly Information Bulletin* to be sold by HMSO and to concern itself with the current business and state of the House. This is an extremely important contribution to solving the problem of knowing what is going on in the House of Commons. Copy is compiled up to Friday afternoons and it is available on Saturdays mornings, certainly by Monday. It tells you the business of the current week and the previous week, gives you a complete alphabetical list of the Bills of the session, together with an indication of how far they have got through Parliament, the same for Private Bills, details of the meetings, witnesses, etc., for Select Committees, the meetings of Standing Committees, a list of European documents received from the Commission and of Green Papers and White Papers. There is a full list of by-elections since the start of the Parliament together with outstanding by-elections and the state of the parties in the House of Commons. There are lists of Principal Ministers and the Shadow Cabinet, and periodically other lists, such as membership of Committees, are published. For a modest subscription libraries can obtain a lot of up to date information. The House of Commons *Weekly Information Bulletin* started at the beginning of session 1978-9.

The Services Committee proposed another annual (possibly sessional) publication which should: 'include statistics about the membership of the House and its Committees, summaries of legislative work (as in the present Public Bill Return) and of Parliamentary Questions, and statistics of sitting hours, etc.'. Much of this information already exists, some of it published in different papers and some of it not. The object is to fit it together into one document and make it available to the public, but this paper, the first number of which will probably be concerned with 1980-81, is at present at the design stage.

The Services Committee further proposed a small educational service for school visits in September and October each year. This service is centred in the Public Information Section and started its work in 1980.

The Public Information Office which is open throughout the year is undoubtedly meeting a real need. Enquiries come in not only by telephone but also by letter from home and abroad. The Section can deal with checking entries about the House of Commons for standard reference works on the one hand and can help individuals who wish to understand the House of Commons or some aspect of its work or membership on the other. Government Departments, newspapers, broadcasting organizations, firms, local authorities, worried constituents, and academics all are found using the service while the rest of the Library staff can concentrate on helping Members. Further, it is the Information Office's responsibility to update and maintain that part of the Post Office's PRESTEL television information service which covers current information on the activities of the House of Commons.

Finally, the Public Information Office prepares two series of publications. The first known as PIO. Series are priced documents obtainable through HMSO and the second series are Factsheets which are available free from the Public Information Office itself (for details see p. 118). Both are of course designed to inform the general public about the working of the House of

Commons and to keep people up-to-date with recent changes. Where the latter are rather technical then the texts are prepared for the layman.

The Sale Office

The Sale Office in the House of Commons was established as long ago as 1836. Before that, the sale of Parliamentary Papers had been in the hands of the Deliverer of the Vote. The Office was put under the control of the energetic Hansard family where it remained until 1886 when the reporting of proceedings was transferred to the publishers, Eyre and Spottiswoode. The Sale Office also came under Eyre and Spottiswoode. Although in 1909 the House of Commons itself took over responsibility for reporting debates, it was not until 1917 that the Sale Office ceased its relationship with Eyre and Spottiswoode. From 1917–64 the Sale Office came under the Secretary of the Speaker but it was then fitted in under the Deliverer of the Vote.

Since 1945, the Sale Office, while continuing to sell Parliamentary Papers to Members who require more copies than their free allocation provides, has mainly sold copies of all types of Parliamentary Papers to the Parliamentary agents employed to promote private legislation, certain embassies, large firms, official and unofficial organizations, and to a few newspapers and indeed individuals. It also receives orders by post from individuals, and, of course, the great advantage of using the service is that all the papers and requests are handled by specialist staff.

In recent evidence to a Select Committee the Deliverer of the Vote indicated that the turnover of the Sale Office has risen from £750 p.a. in 1954 to £40 000 p.a. in 1976[2]. Of this figure of turnover about one third is for standing orders of material supplied and two thirds for individual daily orders from Members and others. The Deliverer pointed out how much faster it was for people abroad to write to the Sale Office than to use HMSO facilities overseas. It was also agreed, however, that the present position of the Sale Office, deep inside the Palace of Westminster where an official pass was needed to gain access to it, precluded it being a useful service to the passing public whose numbers and needs were increasing. It was also thought that the introduction of the broadcasting of Parliamentary debates would increase interest in information about, and the documentation of, Parliament, which a Sale Office more accessible to the public might supply. In order therefore to provide a straight forward over the counter sales point for Parliamentary Papers, the Committee: 'recommended that a public bookstall, to be run by the Sale Office, be sited near St Stephen's porch for the sale of Parliamentary Papers'. They added that it should work closely with the proposed Information Office for the public in the Library Department and be prepared to accept mail orders and orders for the current day's Hansard from visitors to the debates.

At the time of writing, this project has not yet started, but the proposals concerning the Sale Office clearly fit in to a broader policy of Parliament, as an institution, fostering its relations with the public and making information about its work easier to acquire.

Notes

1 *Eighth Report from the Select Committee on House of Commons (Services): Services for the Public.* 1976–7. HC509 vii–viii.

2 *Eighth Report from the Select Committee in House of Commons (Services)* 1976–7 HC 509 p.36 Question 136.

CHAPTER FIVE

House of Lords

The Information Office

I have already described how, following an investigation of the Parliament Office of the House of Lords, the various existing offices concerned with information were, in July 1974, grouped together under a new officer designated the Principal Clerk, Information Services. At the same time a new Information Office was created which was designed to face outwards and to deal with the public's interest in current Parliamentary matters, especially concerning the House of Lords, just as the House of Lords Record Office plays a similar role for the Parliamentary archives.

The establishing of such an information service not only helps the public needing to find out about House of Lords affairs, but it makes it easier for the other offices in the House of Lords, including the Library, to concentrate on their first job which is to serve Members of the House itself. Through co-operation, not only with other offices in the Parliament Office but also with Black Rod's Department, a great number of enquiries are now handled in one place.

The majority of the enquiries come from members of the public, the broadcasting media, the press, government departments, research students, etc. On average about 90 telephone calls a week are received together with an increasing number of letters.

A second group of enquiries is concerned with the checking of up to date information on the House of Lords for the standard reference books. There is the job of checking other information written about Parliament which, in some respects, is quite a fast changing organization. This work may vary from checking a COI reference publication to a major academic treatise.

A third part of the work of the Information Office consists of a weekly summary of business together with certain statistics on the work of the House. This information is circulated to Members etc. – and although it is not printed, copies are available to individual enquirers. A Sessional summary includes an interesting breakdown of the way the House of Lords' time is used. Nothing similar exists for the House of Commons. In addition to this regularly produced information on the working of the House of Lords, which is all available to students and librarians, the House of Lords Information Office has brought out:

1   House of Lords: General Information concerning its History and Procedure. 2nd ed. Feb. 1977 (available on request)
2   Visitors' Guide to the Galleries (given to all those who attend, and on request)
3   The Gentleman Usher of the Black Rod. HMSO 1977
4   The Lord Chancellor. HMSO 1977

More recently a series of House of Lords Fact Sheets have been started and the first six titles are:

1   *House of Lords Reform: 1850–1970* (2nd edition)
2   *The House of Lords and the European Communities* (2nd edition)
3   *Computer Applications in the House of Lords* (2nd edition)
4   *The House of Lords: General Information* [on its history and procedure] (3rd edition)
5   *The Development of Public Information Services at Westminster*
6   *The State Opening of Parliament*

The intention behind these titles is not just to give information, but is also educational (they are available on request from the Information Office, House of Lords) and they will clearly be of value as part of Parliamentary packs of literature it is planned to distribute through the modest educational service being set up within the Information Office in the House of Commons Library.

The House of Lords Information Office is manned by staff of the Parliament Office and this enables them, unlike the more recent House of Commons Information Office, to answer both internal and external questions on procedure. Although the number of enquiries may not be large compared with those received by the House of Commons Library, it has already been proved that there is a very real need for this service to the outside world.

The most recent service to be undertaken by the House of Lords Information Office is the preparation of the *House of Lords Information Bulletin* which like that of the House of Commons appears weekly during the session (starting with session 1978–79) and gives an account of the business of the previous week, the current week and certain future business. There is a list of the state of Bills in the House of Lords for the current session. There is also a list of the European Community proposals which have been referred to the Select Committee on the European Communities indicating to which sub-committee they have gone. The Acts of Parliament and General Synod Measures which have been passed during the session are listed, the reports and the evidence of Select Committees together with Green and White Papers. Each week a breakdown of the House's composition and a list of deaths, introductions to the House, or new peerages are given. This valuable compilation by the Information Office is available either as single copies, by annual subscription or a joint subscription which includes the *House of Commons Weekly Information Bulletin*.

As with the House of Commons, it is the Information Office's responsibility to update and maintain that part of the Post Office's **PRESTEL** television

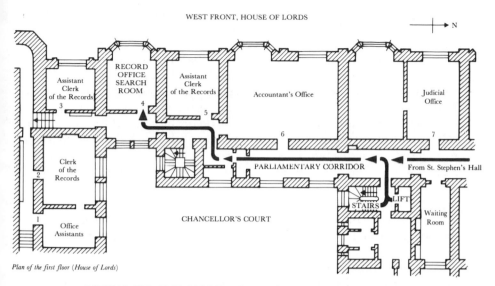

Plan of the first floor (House of Lords)

ACCESS TO THE HOUSE OF LORDS RECORD OFFICE

The House of Lords Record Office may be approached either from the Principal Floor of the Palace *via* the lift or staircase opposite the Clerk of the Parliaments Office, or by the staircase leading from St. Stephen's Hall to the Parliamentary corridor (West Front) on the First Floor. The Search Room is room 4 in this corridor.

information service which covers current information on the activities of the House of Lords.

The Record Office

It was only in 1946 that the House of Lords Record Office was established with a full-time staff and a remit to act as the public record office of the Parliamentary Records. Today, following a generation of hard work, although the number of readers it has space for is limited it is a record office freely open to the public for serious enquiry and research and some thousands of students visit it each year, with perhaps double as many sending written enquiries.

The Record Office is open Mondays to Fridays throughout the year, 9.30 a.m. to 5.30 p.m., and publishes a useful leaflet '*The House of Lords Record Office: General Information*' which is available to researchers free. They are asked if possible to write to the Clerk of the Records in order to indicate the nature of their work and the date of the proposed visit. The standard form of reference to the documents is outlined in the leaflet. There is no charge for this consultation unless the document is required for legal or business purposes when a small charge is made. In order to keep abreast with the accessions to the records reference should be made to the Annual Report of the House of Lords Record Office which is published as a numbered memorandum and is available on demand. The documents added fall into two main groups, namely the official papers and additions to the historical collections.

The official papers which are added each year include from the House of Lords: the *Journal*, Printed and Manuscript Minutes, the Role of the Lords Spiritual and Temporal, certain appeal case material, the original Acts of Parliament, both Public and Local and Personal, together with papers from various offices in both the Parliament Office and Black Rod's Department. A recent addition has been a set of the papers of the European Parliament. The House of Commons similarly sends official papers including the Journal, the order of business and questions sheets and, periodically, papers from the various offices in the Department of the Clerk. Every few years the Public Petitions are sent and from time to time deposits are received from others working in the Palace which range from ceremonial swords to architectural models and drawings. Not all deposits are immediately available to the researcher; normally a restriction of 30 years is placed on confidential items.

Turning to the historical collections, in recent years important collections of modern political papers have been arriving at the Record Office.[1] These include those of Lord Wakehurst, the first Lord Samuel, the fifth Earl of Cadogan, Sir Edward Coates, Rt Hon. Graham White, Lord Stansgate and Lord Sorensen. The most important addition, however, has been the Beaverbrook Library which includes the vast archive of Lloyd George and the papers of Bonar Law and Lord Beaverbrook. This deposit, added to the collections just mentioned, means that the Record Office, in a matter of a few years, has become an important centre for political research. These documents were made available to research students very shortly after receipt.

Since 1946 a great deal of work has gone into the problem of safeguarding and preserving Parliament's Records and all the information they contain. The Victoria Tower has been internally reconstructed and air conditioning introduced. There are now twelve floors maintained at about 60°F and 60 relative humidity. Smoke detectors have been installed together with the latest fire-fighting equipment. One of the floors is loaned to the House of Lords Library and one to the House of Commons Library, otherwise the five or so miles of shelving is mostly devoted to the collections of Parliamentary Records.

Shortly after the War, at the behest of the House of Lords Librarian, Sir Charles Clay, an HMSO bindery was set up in the House of Lords to deal with the binding backlog caused by the War. In addition some manuscript repair was undertaken. Shortly afterwards the technical committee which was concerned with bringing the Victoria Tower up to modern repository standards turned its attention to the documents themselves and in 1950 the conservation programme was extended. The original Acts of Parliament – and that means 25 836 rolls up to 1850 – many volumes of the Journals, the Minutes and Committee Books were cleaned and interleaved with a tissue impregnated with Santobrite. Shortly afterwards, repair work started on thousands of deposited plans, mostly connected with local Acts, which are an important source of local history. To this continuing work was added the cleaning and repair of new collections which arrived, such as the Braye Manuscripts consisting of nearly a thousand items covering the period 1572–1748 which arrived during the years

1947–62. This type of work continues to this day.

In 1951 a start was made on microfilming records beginning with unprinted Private Acts, lest anything should happen to the originals, as there were no copies. In 1958 the microfilming of the main set of House of Lords Papers was begun and by the end of the year those for the period 1499–1692 had been completed. In the 1960s the manuscript Journal of the House of Commons and the Votes and Proceedings were microfilmed while work continued on the great collection of House of Lords Papers. This microfilming work continues today on the collections of both Houses after the documents have been repaired and apart from the microfilm which is kept as an archive duplicate, a copy is made which can be used for making further microfilm copies or prints for the public. The making of microfilm and Xerox photographic copies of the documents at a fixed scale of charges is an important service the Record Office provides. Full details are to be found in the leaflet already mentioned.

The great increase in the number of documents arriving meant that in 1974 space was allocated to the Record Office at Kew for an additional repository. Some 6000 square feet of storage near the new Public Record Office was made available. This has since been increased and by the end of 1978 about 7200 feet of shelving had been erected. Printed material only is sent here and obviously not those documents which require the highest standards of archival storage.

The Record Office has quite an extensive programme of publishing. In addition to the *Calendar of Manuscripts of the House of Lords 1693–1718* published by the House in twelve volumes, and the essential *Guide to the Records of Parliament* by M F Bond; there is a series called House of Lords Record Office Memoranda now totalling 64 in all, which in addition to including the Annual Reports of the Office also includes a series of short studies based on the collection, (see Appendix 3). There are also House of Lords Record Office Occasional Papers which are more substantial studies. The former are available free to students, or if out of print, at the cost of a photocopy. The latter are published by HMSO (see Appendix 3).

Although these documents are part of our history the newest addition to the Record Office's responsibility is very much of our age. In 1978 a special section was started to care for the sound archive of both Houses which followed the introduction of the broadcasting of proceedings in April 1978. With the aid of a staff of four and in specially converted accommodation in the Norman Shaw (South) building, the archive is maintained and made available to Members under the strict control of the two Select Committees on Sound Broadcasting. Each morning the tapes of the previous day's recordings of the debates in the chamber of the House of Commons and House of Lords are delivered by the BBC to the Sound Archives Section of the House of Lords Record Office. One tape equals one hour's debate so that quite frequently a total of a dozen or more tapes may arrive. These are registered, checked, labelled and stored. Access to them is via the published *Hansard* indexes. This works quite well because during this initial stage most requests are through the name of the speaker and as a name index *Hansard*'s is quite good.

Some Standing Committees are also recorded and some Select Committee hearings. When this is happening (the decision is up to the BBC for Standing Committees and the Shorthand Writer for the Select Committees) a red light in the Committee Room indicates to Members that they are being recorded. The quality of these recordings is less good than from the two Chambers. If a Committee wishes not to be recorded, then it must exclude all strangers from its proceedings.

Only Members of either House or officials may listen to these tapes, or the broadcasting authorities which originated the signal. There are three listening booths. In other cases – for instance, overseas broadcasting organizations or institutions at home like the Civil Service College – approval to listen or for a copy to be made must come from the relevant Select Committee on Sound Broadcasting. Evidence was given to the Joint Committee on Sound Broadcasting[2] about the need to select from these records for a permanent archive. So far, however, selection has not taken place and all the tapes received by each House have been kept. As the BBC only keeps about six months of recorded debates, programme producers are having to send requests for earlier tapes to the Parliamentary sound archives.

These are very early days for Parliament's sound archives but clearly it is an important and vivid source for posterity and may well become a growing aspect of current information programmes. Furthermore the Joint Committee emphasized that when funds were available it hoped that the public would have access to the Sound Archives.

Notes

1 See House of Lords Record Office Memorandum No. 60.
2 *Second Report from the Joint Committee on Sound Broadcasting.* 1976–7 HC 284.

CHAPTER SIX

Parliament for the Public

Parliament and the Press

There has always been a certain tension in the relationship between Parliament and the Press. Both compete 'for the claim to be the decisive *vox populi*'.[1] But by linking Parliament and the public, the Press not only reports to its readers on Parliamentary papers and proceedings; conversely it interprets the outside world to Members of both Houses. Therefore in this two-way system, so important in the context of Parliament and Information, for Members to be informed there are the large and well-used press-cuttings collections in the House of Commons Library, while for the public the daily and specialist press is the usual source for learning about the work of Parliament. But historically the reporting of Parliament is really quite a recent development.

'Every person of the Parliament ought to keep secret, and not to disclose, the secrets and things done and spoken in the Parliament house ...'[2] That was the clear position with regard to reporting Parliament in the 1570s and it was confirmed when in 1628 it was resolved not to report speeches in the *Journal*. In 1641 the House of Commons, wishing to secure the support of the citizens of London against Charles I, decided to print various votes and minutes of its proceedings. This regular printing lasted only during these exceptional years and at the Restoration, although unofficial newsletters about Parliament started to circulate in the newly fashionable coffee-houses and the House of Commons decided in 1680 to print its Votes and Proceedings regularly, reporting as we understand it was unknown. In the early eighteenth century the newsletters gave way to the new invention, the newspaper, but after the House of Commons had castigated and imprisoned a number of editors for reporting its proceedings, it was left to the journals to take up Parliamentary reporting, though normally not until the end of the session. The great Dr Johnson, without visiting the Chamber, for some years wrote thundering speeches by Pitt and others for *The Gentleman's Magazine*.

In 1771 John Wilkes, aided by the City of London which this time turned against the House of Commons because of its secrecy, brought the whole subject of reporting to a head. Though the House won its legal case against those who wished to prise open information from Parliament, from this time onwards press reporting of Parliament became more usual and in practice more accepted.

The old House of Commons, which was burnt down in 1834, had no Reporters' Gallery; reporters, if they could get in, were allowed to take notes in the back row of the Strangers' Gallery. But when in 1835 the House of Commons took over temporarily the old House of Lords, as part of the adaptation of that building for their use, a Reporters' Gallery was added and it was here that Charles Dickens worked as a reporter. Barry's Chambers in the new Houses of Parliament included Reporters' Galleries from the beginning.

The Press Gallery is made up of all those whose job is to link what goes on in Parliament with the public outside. It includes therefore *Hansard* staff, who are also House of Lords and House of Commons officials, newspaper and specialist reporters, press agency staff, radio and TV commentators and the Parliamentary Lobby. Some of these, like *Hansard* staff and the press agencies, just report Parliament factually to the public. Others, like the radio and TV commentators and above all the Parliamentary Lobby, not only report Parliament but also interpret it. This means that they try to help us read between the lines of the factual reporting. They reveal the politics behind the proceedings of Parliament.

The Times, Telegraph, Financial Times and *Guardian* make a sustained effort to cover Parliament each day in three different ways. First they give summary reports of debates and selected important Statements and Questions. Whether these make the front headlines or not, they receive significant reporting and this represents for the public some alternative to *Hansard*. Second, there are the Gallery sketch writers who attempt to create the Parliamentary atmosphere, especially the atmosphere of the House of Commons. Third, there are the Lobby correspondents, who aim to penetrate below the surface not just of Parliament but also of Whitehall and to tell us what is really happening and why. (The Lobby correspondents are called such because a limited and controlled number of reporters can have access to the Members' Lobby in the Houses of Parliament and to certain Departmental press conferences where they are given information, mostly on an unattributable basis).

The more popular daily papers cover Parliament in a less systematic way. They have less space for reporting and more transient pressures on that space, but when Parliament becomes the centre of excitment and especially of clashes of personality, which is often the outward sign of clashes of policy, then they will report it and interpret it.

Papers which are published less frequently than daily do not cover the proceedings of Parliament very extensively because by the time they are published the proceedings are often no longer news. They do, however, offer analysis, often by political reporters who are Lobby correspondents.

The present system has grown up over the years and it might be difficult to explain it to a foreign journalist. Undoubtedly Members and the Press need to overlap. In recent years they have acquired a bar in the House of Commons for just this reason, but should there be a more clear-cut relationship? In 1977, when the Services Committee was taking evidence while examining the subject of services for the public, there was an interesting discussion on the subject between the Committee and Mr English MP who came to give evidence. Mr English held very clear views that the House of Commons was not organized to give information to the Press. 'There is now a vast corps of information officers in government Departments servicing the Press and Broadcasting media. There is no equivalent to that for the House of Commons with the result, of course, that many aspects of the work of the House of Commons are relatively ignored.'[3] Mr English proposed that there should be two or three House of Commons Information Officers. At the time, the total number of Information Officers in the Civil Service was 1439.[4] The Chairman of the Committee pointed out that these Civil Servants were trying to promote Departmental policies, while the House of Commons had no policies as such to promote. But some Members were left worried by the total imbalance between the Executive and Parliament in this matter.

Subsequently, the Services Committee made no recommendations on this subject but the new Information Office for the Public, which they recommended should be based in the Library, has received an increasing number of requests for information from the media.

So far we have been considering the reporting of proceedings from the Chambers themselves. The debates in the Standing Committees are also reported on, though in the daily press only if they are the focus of a political clash. But these Standing Committees may have a different type of reporter who represents the specialist press and who may well follow the details of a particular Bill through all its debates on behalf of a specialized paper or journal. This is a growing area responding as it does to the needs of specialist interests.

While reports about Standing Committee work are not extensive, the growth of specialist Select Committees also leads to professional and other journals needing to report on this Parliamentary work. Increasingly, and therefore helping to meet this need, Select Committees take evidence in public. They often publish this evidence on a daily basis so there are regular press reports on the Committee's work as it examines a particular subject. It is also becoming more common for the Chairman of a Select Committee to organize a press conference, generally at the Houses of Parliament, when the time comes for the publication of the Committee's report. The Chairman and other Members of the Committee will endeavour to explain to reporters the background to their report, the information it is based on, and the recommendations they have made to the House.

Quite different is the reporting of Parliament in the local press, often by the local Member himself, and normally of topics which are of local concern. Although this is often a less professional report than those already mentioned, it both helps to keep a local area in touch with Parliament's work and more important their own Member's work, and helps to keep the Member in touch with his constituency.

It is difficult to judge how effective or important the reporting of Parliament by the Press is. When Members of the House of Commons themselves were asked if they used press reports of Parliament,[5] 86 per cent said they did so

regularly, mostly as a prompt to reading *Hansard* itself. Fewer read the press
reports of the House of Lords debates, though it was still an important minority.
But for the general public press reporting must remain important because such
a small number of people can actually attend debates that, despite the recent
introduction of Parliamentary broadcasting, the portrait of Parliament,
whether factual or impressionistic, that comes from the professional journalists
will continue to be the most usual picture of the elected as seen by the electorate.
In a system of Parliamentary democracy it might be said that Members, the
Press and the public all need each other in a three-way link, designed to help
scrutinize our society.

Broadcasting of Parliamentary Proceedings

In 1944 the War Cabinet considered whether broadcasting Parliament would
contribute to an understanding of democracy, for which millions were then
fighting. They saw 'insuperable objections' and thought 'the proceedings in
Parliament were too technical to be understood by the ordinary listener who
would be liable to get a quite false impression of the business transacted'. It
seemed that Parliament was going to be as shy of being broadcast in the
twentieth century as it had been of being reported in the eighteenth.

By the late 1950s the television cameras had nosed their way into the House of
Lords to show us the most handsome of all Parliamentary occasions – the Queen
opening a Parliamentary Session with the speech which she delivers in the
House of Lords.

In 1964–5 the question of broadcasting proceedings was taken up by the
Select Committee on Publications and Debates and the subject was pursued in
1965–6 and 1966–7. The mid-1960s, following the election of 1964, was a period
of Parliamentary reform, the Leader of the House was Richard Crossman, but
in November 1966 the motion to have a trial of closed-circuit TV was rejected
on a free vote by 131 votes to 130. It was the House of Lords which ventured to
use the new technology first and in 1968 there was a short closed-circuit
television experiment and, in the House of Commons in April and May 1968,
there was a sound only experiment.

The House of Commons Services Committee took over the question at this
point and a further experiment took place in 1975. This was the turning point.
The Services Committee considered it a success and on 16 May 1976 the House
of Commons resolved by 299 votes to 124:

> That this House supports the proposal that the public sound broadcasting of its
> proceedings should be arranged on a permanent basis.[6] [Simultaneously the
> House of Lords resolved:] That this House would welcome the public sound
> broadcasting of its proceedings.

A Joint Committee was then set up and it met in May 1976. It started to plan
accommodation and other aspects of the service.

The most important point of principle which had to be decided was whether
Parliament itself would have its own Parliamentary sound broadcasting unit

staffed with its own officials who would play the same role for sound broadcasting that *Hansard* reporters play for the printed debates, or whether it would leave the job to the broadcasting authorities. It decided to hand over the arrangements to the broadcasters, while in February 1978 each House established a Select Committee on Sound Broadcasting to supervise the service and make recommendations to the House. Broadcasting began in April 1978 and shortly afterwards the first Budget was heard. The sound of Members' voices is taken direct from the Tannoy system already existing in the Chambers to enable Members to hear each other and the public in the Strangers' Gallery to hear them. To this is added the sound from extra ceiling microphones which enhance the atmosphere. Combined, these make up the tape which is passed by the BBC each morning to the Parliamentary Sound Archives which I mentioned under the House of Lords Record Office. Independent broadcasting also takes this same 'clean feed' direct for their own broadcasting. In addition, at certain times, there is a commentator in the special boxes providing the necessary linking and elucidation of proceedings.

The BBC broadcast live from the House only especially important events such as Budget speeches. These proceedings are broadcast on Radio 4. Parliamentary Questions on certain days are distributed in recorded form to the local radio in London, Medway and Bristol. Individual local radio stations and regions may broadcast items of particular interest to their area, e.g. Northern Ireland Questions. Maybe the first sound broadcast of historic importance was the debate on the motion of 'no confidence' tabled by the Opposition on 28 March 1979, which they won by 311 votes to 310. For the first time the public could share in the intense excitement of the climax and the following moment of quiet when it was realized the Government had fallen and the Prime Minister commented 'Mr Speaker, now that the House of Commons has declared itself, we shall take our case to the country'.

One of the jobs of the BBC is to sub-edit the tapes and then package them for use in network broadcasts, or for one of the twenty local radio stations, for the eight English TV regions, or for radio or TV in the regions of Scotland, Wales and Northern Ireland. This editing would include sending Parliamentary Questions which relate to a particular area to the local radio station. Where there is a debate on a general subject which is of special relevance to certain areas – race relations for instance – then relevant tapes are sent out. They are transmitted to these various stations direct from the Norman Shaw (South) building through Broadcasting House. The decision as to whether to use this material rests with the local producers.

Following the 1944 decision against broadcasting Parliament, it was agreed that a programme called 'Today in Parliament' should be started. This ran for fifteen minutes, but now that the programme can be interspersed with the spoken word from Members themselves, it has been lengthened to thirty minutes. 'Yesterday in Parliament', which is a little shorter, is a further sub-editing of the previous night's 'Today in Parliament', together with any important matters which may have taken place in Parliament after the making of 'Today in Parliament' the previous evening. Parliamentary proceedings form an important source for network news broadcasts and also for current affairs programmes. Clearly it will take time to establish the extent to which listeners and viewers will respond to the use of this material. In time also there will be a completely different use of those tapes which are kept permanently, as they will develop both a period interest and a biographical interest for future historians and makers of historical programmes.

It is not only the proceedings in the two Houses of Parliament which may be broadcast. Many Select Committees are also recorded, and when recordings are made, a red light glows so that Members know that they may be 'on the air'. If the Committee go into a closed session and the public are excluded, the sound feed to the broadcasters is terminated. Similarly, the proceedings of Standing Committees can be recorded. Because of the shape and layout of committee rooms and the nature of the equipment, the quality of these transmissions is not as good as those from the Chambers themselves.

The BBC organization at Westminster is a large one, including commentators in the box, reporters in the gallery, a mixing unit actually in the Palace of Westminster; and farther away in the Norman Shaw (South) building there are two studios, an editorial area comprising four separate editorial desks which cover network radio news, including 'Today in Parliament' and 'Yesterday in Parliament', local radio and the regions, network radio current affairs and network television news. Eight master tapes can be produced simultaneously (usually three House of Lords and five House of Commons) and one set of these tapes of each House is passed to the Parliamentary Archives.

For commercial broadcasting, Independent Radio News acts as the provider of both commentary on and broadcasts of Parliamentary proceedings. These tapes are distributed, some regularly and some by request, to the commercial radio and the commercial TV companies.

The IRN has reporters in the Chamber of both Houses and the proceedings and commentary are 'mixed' in the Norman Shaw (South) building. They use the same signal for the broadcasts as the BBC. Regular programmes include afternoon and night summaries of Parliament's work of three to four minutes which are distributed to all stations and a fifteen-minute programme for LBC itself each evening. IRN does not use news readers but political reporters who create the whole programme themselves. They receive and respond to regional broadcasting's initiative in requesting tapes, much in the same way as the BBC responds to their regional producers' requests for particular tapes.

It is too early yet to estimate the impact of the broadcasting of Parliamentary proceedings on the public. But two or three generalizations can be risked.

The first is that there can be little doubt that, especially in regional and local broadcasts, actually to hear your local Member raising a local question with a Minister is far more effective than reading about it in the press. There is colour in the human voice pressing a Minister or pleading a cause, which has a much greater impact than reading it in a newspaper. There is also the question of the aural recognition of a Member, the way in which his voice becomes well known through the local radio in the district which he represents. The importance of this may not yet have been recognized by all Members themselves. The second impact is that it conveys very quickly the great range and changing mood of Parliament, especially of the House of Commons. Sound broadcasting can convey the human quality of the institution very vividly. For instance, after a routine and probably noisy Question Time, there might follow a Statement on a mining tragedy. A Welsh Member may rise and speak of the families of the victims with the strong feelings of an ex-miner. The House of Commons will suddenly draw together in its silent sympathy. No written report could so effectively convey Members' response.

The third impact will be very difficult to measure. It is the question of whether Parliament will become a more important imparter of information to the general public. In the nineteenth century official publishing was really synonymous with Parliamentary publishing and the relatively small literate group which ran society would certainly find themselves well read in Parliamentary proceedings and publications. Blue books were reviewed at length in the journals. It will be interesting to see whether through sound broadcasting Parliament will be able to reassert its position as an important centre of information for our more diffuse and democratic age.

Notes

1 Hansard Society. *Parliamentary Reform*, 1961, 197.
2 Mountmorres 'History ... of the Irish Parliament' 2 vol., Reprinted with introduction by D.J.T. Englefield. 1971. 1. 143.
3 *Eighth Report for the Services Committee: Services for the Public*. 1976-7 HC 509. 68.
4 *Eighth Report for the Services Committee: Services for the Public*. 1976-7 HC 509. 67.
5 Barker, A. and Rush, M. The Member of Parliament and his Information. 1970, pp.136-7.
6 *House of Commons Journal* **232**. 214.

Conclusion

By the time this book appears each of us will have had a chance to contribute our own political opinion to the election of the forty-eighth Parliament of the United Kingdom of Great Britain and Northern Ireland. The House of Commons will have returned to the electorate for the most fundamental piece of information Parliament ever receives: what does the electorate see as the priorities for our society? What will be the political persuasion of the majority of the House of Commons?

Recent Parliaments, and especially the forty-seventh elected in October 1974, have worked hard to improve their methods of informing Parliament and of informing the public about Parliament. *Parliament and Information* is an attempt, among other things, to report on this. But it is clear that the present Parliament will see the further development of many aspects of this problem. Computer power is only just starting to be put at the service of Members of both Houses. Now that arguments are over concerning the principle and details of broadcasting Parliament's proceedings, it is likely that April 1978 will be seen as an important date in the relationship of Parliament and the public, maybe even of the development of democracy in this country. Now that we have routine sound broadcasting, can TV be far behind? Of more immediate concern to the House of Commons itself is the 1978 Select Committee Report on Procedure. While not sweeping in its proposals, it does seek through practical propositions to adjust the balance between the growing power of the Executive and the declining strength of Parliament. And it does so by asserting:

> What is required is an acceptance by the House – and by the country at large – of the urgent need to provide Members with adequate assistance in performing the increased work required of them ... but the House must recognise that unless Members are provided with information services and staff support capable of relieving them of much of the routine and essential preparatory work, they will not be able to do this work properly whether under present arrangements or under the changes we propose.[1]

A further development which will continue into the forty-eighth Parliament will be the changes in the administration of the staff of the House of Commons itself, which follows on the passing of the House of Commons (Administration) Act 1978. There is, too, from the viewpoint of information, the question of the possible addition of more specialist staff, especially for Select Committees, and of the growing specialization of staff within the Library Department.

We must not forget the position of Members themselves, not only their slowly growing personal staff, which is a new element in the provision of information and other support, not only the question of their electors, now also voting for the European Parliament, but also how they see their role, how much they are paid, etc., their personal status and consequently that of Parliament itself. Worried commentators indeed suggest that Parliament's own self-confidence may be the key to its future development.

All these are factors which will certainly affect Westminster in the coming years but, in an institution where precedent is so important, the last word concerning 'Parliament and Information' must rest with history, with Thomas Vardon who started his career as the first House of Commons Sub-Librarian in Soane's new library in 1828. In 1831 Benjamin Spiller, the first Librarian, died while still in his post, Vardon inherited the Librarianship, and a young man called Erskine May succeeded to the Sub-Librarian post. Three years later Vardon's Library was burnt down. During this period the Reform Act was passed, the number of Members using the Library trebled and the number of Parliamentary Papers quickly grew. The whole setting presented a dynamic and new challenge and when Vardon, five months after the fire, appeared to give evidence before a Select Committee, he had carefully worked out detailed accommodation needs for the rebuilding of the House of Commons Library. It was an important committee he appeared before – the Standing Committee on the Library – and it included Mr Speaker in the Chair, the Chancellor of the Exchequer and a young Member called W E Gladstone. With his third question the Speaker gave the well-prepared Vardon a unique opening. He seized it:

> 3. How do you distinguish the duties of attending as a librarian to the Parliamentary Library from the duties of attending any other public library? The distinction is very strong in practice when properly worked out. My duties, as attending the parliamentary department of the Library, I consider to embrace the attendance on Members generally, or select committees specially, and upon the House during the progress of public business. The attendance on Members generally is rather indefinite, but it amounts in fact to this, that to the extent of time which I can give, which is day and night during the sitting of the House, the practice is, that there is no subject connected with parliamentary business, on finance, or the forms of the House, or the progress of Bills, or the contents of Acts, on which I am not called upon to afford instant information. In respect to select committees, the notes continually sent me from the Chairmen or members of Committees do not specify 'I want such and such a volume of such a work', but their notes contain generally queries whether there be law upon such and such a subject; if there be, where it can be found; in what Acts: or regarding parliamentary papers, whether such information can be given, and whether, without troubling the Members with long papers, I can state briefly the information desired in their queries, which of course involves a great deal of indefinite labour during the whole of the day. Then, to the House at night, every

Member must be aware of the sort of applications which are made to the Librarians, by the minute, I may almost say, for the debates, or the divisions which have taken place on particular occasions; for information concerning Finance Papers, Trade or Acts of Parliament relating to the subject under discussion, etc.: this necessarily involves (and it cannot possibly be stopped) a great deal of conversation, which must take place between the Members and the Librarians. The communications with select committees involve the attendance of messengers or committee clerks, and therefore, it is impossible to keep the Parliamentary Library quiet, their applications necessarily creating noise; add also, that by the recommendation of different select committees, Members have been requested to apply to the Library on moving for papers or accounts, in order to avoid the multiplication of printing by asking for information already before the House; and that, since the report of the Committee on Public Documents, all papers not ordered to be printed are deposited in the Library for the use of the House; and the Committee will see the reason why I distinguish between the parliamentary duties of the librarian and those which would more particularly attach to a literary library.

Nearly 150 years later, despite the changes in technology, it is in many respects difficult to improve on his reply.

Appendix One

Addresses, Forms of Address, Telephone Numbers etc. in the Houses of Parliament and a Parliamentary Bookshelf

ADDRESSES, FORM OF ADDRESS, TELEPHONE NUMBERS ETC.

Address

House of Lords   LONDON SW1A 0PW

House of Commons   LONDON SW1A 0AA

Form of address

(a)   Lords, Temporal

Duke/Duchess — The Most Noble[1] the D...

[Nowadays it is more common for those in correspondence with Dukes to use the prefix 'His Grace the D...']

Marquis/Marchioness — The Most Honourable the M...

Earl/Countess — The Right Honourable the Earl/Countess...

Viscount/Viscountess — The Right Honourable the V...

Baron/Baroness/Lady — The Right Honourable the Lord ...

The Right Honourable the Baroness ...

The Right Honourable the Lady...

In Parliamentary and social correspondence prefixes may be omitted, thus:

The Duke of ...

The Earl of ...

The Baroness ... of ...

(NB. In this case 'The Rt Hon.' is used to indicate membership of the Privy Council.)

(b)   Lords, Spiritual

Archbishops — The Most Reverend and Right Honourable the Lord Archbishop of Canterbury/York

(NB. Both Archbishops are Privy Councillors.)

Bishop of London — The Right Reverend and Right Honourable the Lord Bishop of London

(NB. The Bishop of London is a Privy Councillor.)

Bishops — The Right Reverend the Lord Bishop of ...

(NB. Only some Bishops are members of the House of Lords.)

(c)   Members of Parliament   The initials MP are placed at the
                                                end of any list of qualifications,
                                                decorations, etc.
                                       If a Member is a Privy Councillor the
                                       'The Right Honourable' or 'Rt Hon.'
                                   precedes the name and MP follows as above.

Information about Parliament

(a)   House of Lords (General and Procedure). The Information Office, House
       of Lords: 01–219 3107, 5454 or 5428 during session: 01–219 3074
       during recess.

(b)   House of Lords and House of Commons (Parliamentary Records). The
       Record Office, House of Lords: 01–219 3074

(c)   House of Commons (General and Current Information). Public
       Information Office, The Library: 01–219 4272/4

(d)   House of Commons (Technical Procedural matters) Journal Office,
       House of Commons: 01–219 3361

Evidence for Parliament

(a)   House of Lords. Clerk of the Committee Office, House of Lords:
       01–219 3218
       Clerk of the European Communities Committee, House of Lords:
       01–219 3130

(b)   House of Commons. Clerk of Select Committees, House of Commons:
       01–219 5562, 4300

PARLIAMENTARY BOOKSHELF

Procedure etc.

Abraham, L.A. and Hawtrey, S.C. *Parliamentary Dictionary*, 3rd ed., 1970
Central Office of Information *The British Parliament* (Ref. Pam.33), 1978 and
       Supplement 1979
House of Commons Manual of Procedure in the Public Business 11th ed. 1974
House of Commons Standing Orders ... Public Business 1976
House of Lords Companion to the Standing Orders ... 1979
House of Lords Standing Orders ... Public Business 1976 (amended 1977)
May, Sir T. Erskine *The Law, Privileges, Proceedings and Usage of Parliament*, 19th
       ed., 1976
Rush, M. and Shaw, M. *The House of Commons: Services and Facilities*, 1974
Taylor, E. *The House of Commons at Work*, 9th ed., 1979
Wilding, N. and Laundy, P. *An Encyclopaedia of Parliament*, 4th ed., 1972

Members (Lists and Biographies)

BBC Guide to Parliament, 1979
Dod's Parliamentary Companion 1832 – (Published annually, often with extra
       edition after election)
Hansard (House of Commons) First issue of each session lists Members

History of Parliament Trust (in progress) 1715-54 2 vols.; 1754-90 3 vols.
  Biographies of MPs.
House of Lords Roll of the Lords Spiritual and Temporal published the first day
  of each session by HMSO
Political Companion (Published six-monthly)
Roth, A. The MPs Chart, 1980
Times Guide to the House of Commons 1929 - (Published after each election:
includes   photographs.)
Vacher's Parliamentary Companion 1832 - (published quarterly).
Who's Who 1897 - (Published annually: includes all MPs).

The Houses of Parliament

Bond, M. *The Houses of Parliament,* 1973
Fell, Sir B. *The Houses of Parliament,* 13th ed., 1977
History of the King's Works 1066-1851, 6 volumes. (Parts covering the Palace of
  Westminster)
Pope-Hennessy, James *The Houses of Parliament,* 1974
Port, M. H. *The Houses of Parliament,* 1976 (the major work of reference)
Taylor, E. *The Houses of Parliament,* 1976

Journals

The House Magazine (weekly during session)
Parliamentary Affairs (quarterly)
The Parliamentarian (quarterly)
The Table (annually)

Appendix Two

Visiting the Palace of Westminster

WESTMINSTER HALL

Westminster Hall is open to the public who should enter via New Palace Yard. During Sessions, weekdays 10.00 a.m.-1.30 p.m. provided neither House is sitting, and during Recesses 10.00a.m.-4.00 p.m. Saturdays, 10.00 a.m.-5.00 p.m. Sundays closed.

PALACE OF WESTMINSTER

The Palace of Westminster is open to the public who should enter at the Norman Porch, House of Lords, near the Victoria Tower on Saturdays (except the Saturday immediately preceding the State Opening of a new Session of Parliament), Easter Monday and the following Tuesday, May Day Bank Holiday, Spring Bank Holiday and the following Tuesday, Summer Bank Holiday and the following Tuesday, August Mondays, Tuesdays and Thursdays, and September Thursdays. Admission is from 10.00 a.m. to 4.30 p.m. Sundays closed.

ATTENDING A DEBATE IN THE HOUSE OF COMMONS OR THE HOUSE OF LORDS

Parliamentary debates are open to the public who should join the appropriate queue at St Stephen's entrance.

House of Commons: Mondays–Thursdays, House meets 2.30 p.m., the head of the queue is not normally admitted until 4.15 p.m. Friday, House meets 9.30 a.m.

House of Lords: Tuesdays, Wednesdays, House meets 2.30 p.m., Thursdays 3.00 p.m.; some Mondays 2.30 p.m., and occasional Fridays 11.00 a.m.

Members of each House of Parliament may be applied to well in advance for accelerated admittance. Overseas visitors may obtain Cards of Introduction from their Embassy or High Commission. Printed information explaining the lay-out, procedure and business of the day is handed to all visitors.

ATTENDING A STANDING COMMITTEE DEBATE OR SELECT COMMITTEE HEARING

Standing Committee debates are open to the public and in practice are confined to the House of Commons. They are the debates by Members on the detailed aspects of legislation covering Amendments, New Clauses etc. The Committee Room is arranged as a miniature House of Commons and details of sittings are to be found in the *House of Commons Weekly Information Bulletin*. They generally sit on Tuesday, Wednesday and Thursday mornings 10.30 a.m.–1.00 p.m. and a verbatim report *Hansard* of the proceedings is available.

Select Committee hearings of evidence are mostly open to the public, though not 'domestic' Committees like the Services Committee or the Procedure Committee. The Committee Room is arranged in a horseshoe and oral evidence is taken from witnesses who are questioned. Details of sittings in public are to be found in the *House of Commons Weekly Information Bulletin* and also a few newspapers. Select Committees sit in the morning, in the afternoon and sometimes in the evening. The Select Committees normally order the evidence to be published, sometimes day by day and sometimes later with the report and it appears as a House of Commons paper.

In the House of Lords the Select Committee on European Communities together with its sub-committees is open to the public and details of its sittings are to be found in the *House of Lords Weekly Information Bulletin*.

SCHOOL VISITS TO PARLIAMENT

A limited number of school visits by older children are organized by the Education Officer of the House of Commons Library Department. The visit includes an audio-visual presentation on Parliament and a conducted tour of the Palace of Westminster. For details schools should write to the Education Officer, House of Commons Library, Norman Shaw (South), London SW1A 0AA, or telephone 01–219 4750.

Appendix Three

List of Parliamentary Papers and of Publications Prepared at the Houses of Parliament

PARLIAMENT

The Public General Acts and General Synod Measures	HMSO
The Local and Personal Acts	HMSO

HOUSE OF LORDS

Minutes of Proceedings	HMSO
Journal	HMSO
Papers and Bills	HMSO
Parliamentary Debates (Hansard)	HMSO
Weekly Information Bulletin	HMSO
A Guide for Visitors to the Galleries	

Information Office

Fact-sheets
  House of Lords Reform: 1850-1970 (2nd edition).
  The House of Lords and the European Communities (2nd edition).
  Computer Applications in the House of Lords (2nd edition).
  The House of Lords: General information concerning its history and procedure (3rd edition); statistics of the House's business in the 1977-78 session are now available with this fact-sheet.
  The Development of Public Information Services at Westminster.
  The State opening of Parliament.
Publication Series

Gentleman Usher of the Black Rod	HMSO
Lord Chancellor	HMSO
Works of Art in the House of Lords, edited by Maurice Bond	HMSO

Record Office

Guide to the Records of Parliament by M.F. Bond	HMSO
Calendar of the Manuscripts of the House of Lords 1450-1693 were included in the appendices to the Reports of the Historical Manuscripts Commission	

(1450–1678) Reports 1–9, these are reprinted by Kraus,
and (1678–1693) Reports 11–14.
Calendar of the Manuscripts of the House of Lords (1693–1718), 12
volumes.   HMSO
Occasional Publications
  Diaries and Papers of Sir Edward Dering 1644–84   HMSO
  Divisions in the House of Lords: an analytical list, 1685–1857   HMSO
Memoranda
Those Memoranda in the following list which are not marked as being out of
print are available free to students and others applying to the Clerk of the
Records at the House of Lords:

1   *Select List of Classes of Records in the House Of Lords Record Office*, (revised ed.,
    1973).
2   *Report of the House of Lords Record Office, 1950.* (1951) *out of print.*
3   *The House of Lords Calendar of Manuscripts.* (1960) *out of print.*
4   *Catalogue of Display of Parliamentary Archives, 1951*, (1951) *out of print.*
5   *Report of the House of Lords Record Office, 1951.* (1952) *out of print.*
6   *Analysis of Current Papers deposited in the Record Office.* (1952) *out of print.*
7   *The Braye Manuscripts.* (1952) *out of print.*
8   *Report of the House of Lords Record Office, 1952.* (1953) *out of print.*
9   *Catalogue of the Display of Manuscripts.* (1953) *out of print.*
10 *Report of the House of Lords Record Office, 1953, (1954) out of print.*
11 *The Braye Manuscripts sold at Messrs. Christie, 23 June 1954.* (1954) *out of
    print.*
12 *Report of the House of Lords Record Office, 1954.* (1955) *out of print.*
13 *The Journals, Minutes and Committee Books of the House of Lords.* (Revised ed.,
    1957).
14 *Report of the House of Lords Record Office, 1955.* (1956).
15 *Report of the House of Lords Record Office, 1956.* (1957) *out of print.*
16 *The Private Bill Records of the House of Lords.* (1957) *out of print.*
17 *Report of the House of Lords Record Office, 1957.* (1958) *out of print.*
18 *Guide to the Parliament Office Papers.* (1958) *out of print.*
19 *Report of the House of Lords Record Office, 1958.* (1959) *out of print.*
20 *Guide to the House of Lords Papers and Petitions.* (1959).
21 *Report of the House of Lords Record Office, 1959.* (1960) *out of print.*
22 *Clerks in the Parliament Office, 1600–1900.* (1960) *out of print.*
23 *Report of the House of Lords Record Office, 1960.* (1961) *out of print.*
24 *The Braye Manuscripts bought by the Record Office on 26 January 1961.* (1961)
    out of print.
25 *The Use of Finding Aids in the Record Office Search Room.* (Revised ed., 1972).
26 *Hand List of Paintings, Drawings and Engravings, etc., of the House of Lords and
    House of Commons. 1523–1900.* (Revised ed., 1972).
27 *Report of the House of Lords Record Office, 1961.* (1962) *out of print.*
28 *Report of the House of Lords Record Office, 1962.* (1963) *out of print.*

29   *Catalogue of the Records of Parliament displayed at the Opening of the Victoria Tower Repository by The Right Honourable the Viscount Hailsham, 3 July 1963.* (1963).
30   *Report of the House of Lords Record Office, 1963.* (1964).
31   *Leaders and Whips in The House of Lords, 1783-1964.* (1964).
32   *Report of the House of Lords Record Office, 1964.* (1965).
33   *Further Materials from an Unpublished Manuscript of the Lords Journal for Sessions 1559 and 1597 to 1598.* (1965).
34   *Report of the House of Lords Record Office, 1965.* (1966).
35   *The Political Papers of Herbert, 1st Viscount Samuel.* (Revised ed., 1974).
36   *Report of the House of Lords Record Office, 1966.* (1967).
37   *The Financial Administration and Records of the Parliament Office, 1824 to 1868.* (1967).
38   *Report of the House of Lords Record Office, 1967.* (1968).
39   *A List of Representative Peers for Scotland, 1707 to 1963, and for Ireland 1800 to 1961.* (1968).
40   *Report of the House of Lords Record Office, 1968.* (1969).
41   *Literary and Scientific Papers of Herbert, 1st Viscount Samuel.* (1969).
42   *Report of the House of Lords Record Office, 1969.* (1970).
43   *Letters and Diaries of Speaker Brand, 1855-1892.* (1970).
44   *Report of the House of Lords Record Office, 1970.* (1971).
45   *Officers of the House of Lords, 1485-1971.* (1971).
46   *Report of the House of Lords Record Office, 1971.* (1972). *out of print.*
47   *Letters of the Second Earl of Tweeddale, 1672 to 1692.* (1972).
48   *Report of the House of Lords Record Office, 1972.* (1973).
49   *Handlist of the Papers of Reginald, Lord Sorensen (the Rev. R.W. Sorensen, M.P.).* (1973).
50   *Sources for Economic History amongst the Parliamentary Records in the House of Lords Record Office.* (1973).
51   *Report of the House of Lords Record Office, 1973.* (1974).
52   *The Origin of the Office of Chairman of Committees in the House of Lords.* (1974).
53   *Report of the House of Lords Record Office, 1974.* (1975).
54   *A Guide to the Political Papers, 1874-1970, deposited by the First Beaverbrook Foundation.* (1975).
55   *Report of the House of Lords Record Office, 1975.* (1976).
60   *A Guide to the Historical Collections of the nineteenth and twentieth centuries preserved in the House of Lords Record Office* (1978).
61   *Report of the House of Lords Record Office, 1978.* (1979).
62   *An Exhibition of the Records of Parliament in the Royal Gallery, House of Lords.* (1979).
63   *Report of the House of Lords Record Office, 1979.* (1980).
64   *Parliamentary functions of the Sovereign since 1509.* (1980).

Unnumbered: *A Handlist of Articles in periodicals and other serial publications relating to the History of Parliament* (1973).

> *The House of Lords Record Office Technical Services.* (1975).
> *The Parliament Office in the seventeenth and eighteenth centuries.* (1977).
> *Short guide to the Records of Parliament (3rd edition)* (1979)

Xerox copies of out of print Memoranda can be supplied at current photocopying charges.

There is also available, free, on application to the Clerk of the Records at the House of Lords Record Office, London, SW1A 0PW, a leaflet of General Information concerning the use of the office by members of the public.

HOUSE OF COMMONS

Vote	HMSO
Journal	HMSO
House of Commons and Command Papers and Bills	HMSO
Parliamentary Debates (Hansard)	HMSO
Standing Committee Debates	HMSO
Weekly Information Bulletin	HMSO
A Guide for Visitors to the Galleries	
Standing Orders of the House of Commons: Public Business, 1979	HMSO

Library

Documents

1	*Acts of Parliament. some Distinctions in their Nature and Numbering*	1955	HMSO
2	*A Bibliography of Parliamentary Debates of Great Britain*	1967 (reprinted)	HMSO HMSO
3	*The Mace in the House of Commons*	1971 (revised)	HMSO HMSO
4	*Official Dress worn in the House of Commons*	1977 (reprinted)	HMSO HMSO
5	*Access to Subordinate Legislation*	1963	HMSO
6	*Ceremonial in the House of Commons*	1967 (reprinted)	HMSO HMSO
7	*The Journal of the House of Commons: a Bibliographical and Historical Guide*	1971	HMSO
8	*Votes and Standing Orders of the House of Commons: The Beginning*	1971	HMSO
9	*Erskine May's Private Journal 1857–1882: Diary of a Great Parliamentarian*	1971	HMSO
10	*William Lambarde's Notes on the Procedures and Privileges of the House of Commons* (1584)	1977	HMSO

11 *Ceremonial and the Mace in the*   1980   HMSO
     House of Commons (updated and consolidated
     edition of nos. 3, 4 and 6)
Public Information Series (Priced documents)
     Questions in the House   HMSO
     The Attlee Memorial Statue   HMSO
     The Great Clock (Big Ben) (in preparation)
     Ceremonial and Dress in the Commons (in preparation)
Fact-sheets (available on request)
     Parliamentary stages of a Government Bill
     Outlawries Bill
     Private Members' Bill
     Procedural Changes of 31 October 1979
     Women in the House of Commons
     The New Departmental Select Committee structure
     All-Party Subject Groups in the House of Commons

$\mathscr{A}ppendix \mathscr{F}our$

List of annual reports which are laid before Parliament but which are not to be found among the Sessional Papers

One of the traditional ways for Parliament to acquire information has been to insist that when an organization is set up under an Act it should report annually to Parliament. This is not only essential for Parliament's oversight of its work but it is also an important source of information for the public. In nearly all cases if this informaton is presented to Parliament by command it is published as a Command Paper. If, however, it is laid before Parliament under a statute then it is an Act paper and requires an order to print by the House of Commons. If the House of Commons orders it to be printed these House of Commons Papers and the Command Papers already mentioned are to be found among the printed Sessional Papers and can be bought from HMSO. They will appear in Part I of the index to the *House of Commons Journal*, in the Sessional Index and its cumulations and in the HMSO Daily List and the monthly and annual catalogues of Government publications.

In recent years however a large number of papers laid before Parliament have ceased to be ordered to be printed by the House of Commons; indeed the decision whether a paper will or will not be printed now rests with the government Department not with the House of Commons. This represents a serious deterioration in the bibliographical control of Parliamentary papers. The papers will of course continue to appear in Part I of the index to the *House of Commons Journal* because they must continue to be laid before Parliament. This however is the only comprehensive bibliographical control which remains and as the *House of Commons Journal* costs nearly one hundred pounds and is available in relatively few libraries most librarians and many researchers will not have access to it easily. If they are not ordered to be printed then they will not appear in the Sessional Index nor will they be among the Sessional Papers. (Both the index of the *House of Commons Journal* and Sessional Index are generally a few sessions in arrears.)

If an organization decides to use HMSO either to print and publish its annual report or alternatively to distribute it, then the report will appear in HMSO catalogues. If the institution decides to publish another way or not to publish at all then the only source for the annual report is the organization itself. Most of this material does not appear regularly in BNB.

I have tried to list below the annual reports which are laid before Parliament but which are now (sessions 1977-8) not to be found among the Sessional Papers. Some have ceased to be among the Sessional Papers, some have never been among them. Whichever it is they represent a group of materials which cause libraries and researchers considerable headaches. Those which ceased to be Sessional Papers in the decade 1959/60-1968/69 are noted in the Decennial Index which covers this period. It is very much to be hoped that when the Decennial Index of the Sessional papers for the decade of the seventies is prepared, that it similarly will be annotated if annual reports have ceased to be among the Sessional Papers.

The list is arranged alphabetically under the name of the body reporting or the Act under which a report must be made. An asterisk means the report appears in government publications and is available from HMSO.

Advisory, Conciliation and Arbitration Service
Agricultural Horticultural & Forestry Industry Training Board
Anglian Water Authority
Apple and Pear Development Council
British Aerospace
*British Airports Authority
*British Airways Board
*British Broadcasting Corporation
*British Gas Corporation
British Library
*British National Oil Corporation
British Nuclear Fuels Ltd
*British Railways Board
British Shipbuilders Ltd
*British Steel Corporation
   Annual Reports and Accounts
   Constituent Companies' Reports
British Tourist Authority
British Transport Docks Board
*British Waterways Board
*Cable and Wireless
Carpet Industry Training Board
Central Arbitration Committee
Central Council for Agricultural and Horticultural Corporation
*Central Electricity Generating Board
Ceramics Glass & Minerals Products Industry Training Board
Chemical & Allied Products Industry Training Board
Church Commissioners
Civil Air Transport Industry Training Board

Civil Aviation Authority
Clothing Industry Training Board
Commonwealth Development Corporation
*Companies report by the Department of Trade
Construction Industry Training Board
Council on Tribunals
*Countryside Commission (Scotland)
Covent Garden Market Authority
*Crofters Commission
*Crown Estates Commissioners
Distributive Industry Training Board
East Midlands Gas Consumers' Council
*Eastern Electricity Board
*Education and Science, Ministers' Annual Report
Education (Wales) Report by Secretary of State on schools in Wales
Eggs Authority
Electricity Act 1947 and 1957
Electricity Council
Engineering Industry Training Board
English Tourist Board
*Equal Opportunities Commission
Food Drink & Tobacco Industry Training Board
Footwear etc. Industry Training Board
*Friendly Societies Reports of Chief Registrar Parts 1-3
Furniture & Timber Industry Training Board
Furniture Development Council
Gas Industry Training Board
General Nursing Council (England and Wales)
General Nursing Council (Scotland)
General Pier and Harbour Acts 1861-1915 Report by Minister of Agriculture
    Report by Secretary of State for Environment
*Herring Industry Board
*Highlands and Islands Development Board
Home-Grown Cereals Authority
Horserace Betting Levy Board
Horserace Totalisator Board
Hosiery and Allied Trades Research Association
Hotel & Catering Industry Training Board
*Housing Corporation
Independent Broadcasting Authority
*Insurance Companies Act 1974 Report by Secretary of State for Trade
Iron & Steel Industry Training Board
Knitting Lace & Net Industry Training Board
*Legal Aid and Advice (Scotland)
*London Electricity Board

Man-made Fibre Industry Training Board
Manpower Services Commission
Meat and Livestock Commission
Merchant Shipping Act 1906 Report on exemptions
Merseyside and North Wales Electricity Board
*Midlands Electricity Board
*National Bus Company
*National Coal Board
National Enterprise Board
National Freight Corporation
*National Galleries (Scotland)
National Gas Consumers' Council
*National Museum of Antiquities (Scotland)
National Ports Council
National Research Development Corporation
National Water Council
North of Scotland Hydro-Electric Board
North Thames Gas Consumers' Council
*North-Eastern Electricity Board
North-Eastern Gas Consumers' Council
Northern Gas Consumers' Council
Northumbrian Water Authority
*North-West Water Authority
*North-Western Electricity Board
North-Western Gas Consumers' Board
Oil and Gas Annual Development Report
Paper and Paper Products Industry Training Board
Petroleum Industry Training Board
Port of London Authority
*Post Office
Prevention of Oil Pollution Act 1971 Report on the exercise of functions by the
    Department of Trade
Printing and Publishing Industry Training Board
*Public Works Loan Board
Radiochemical Centre Ltd
*Red Deer Commission
Redundant Churches Fund
*Registrar General for Scotland's Report
*Registrar General's Report
Roads in Wales
Road Transport Industry Training Board
Rubber and Plastics Processing Industry Training Board
Scottish Gas Consumers' Council
Scottish Health Service Planning Council
Scottish National Camps Association Ltd

Scottish Tourist Board
Scottish Transport Group
Sea Fisheries (Shellfish) Act 1967 Report by Minister of Agriculture
Severn-Trent Water Authority
Shipbuilding Industry Training Board
Smallholdings (England and Wales)
*South of Scotland Electricity Board
South Wales Electricity Board
South-Eastern Electricity Board
South-Eastern Gas Consumers' Council
South-West Electricity Board
South-West Water Authority
South-Western Gas Consumers' Council
Southern Electricity Board
Southern Gas Consumers' Council
Southern Water Authority
*Sugar Board
Thames Water Authority
Transport Tribunal
*UK Atomic Energy Authority
Wales Gas Consumers' Council
Wales Tourist Board
Water Authorities
Water Space Amenity Commission
Welsh National Water Development Authority
Welsh Water Authority
Wessex Water Authority
West Midlands Gas Consumers' Council
*White Fish Authority
Wool Industry Research Association
Wool etc Industry Training Board
*Yorkshire Electricity Board
Yorkshire Water Authority

Appendix Five

List of Select and Standing Committees of Parliament

As has already been described, much of the work of Parliament takes place in Select, and in the case of the House of Commons Standing Committees. Below are listed the main Committees of both Houses of Parliament. The Reports and Evidence etc. of these Committees is published as a House of Lords or House of Commons Paper as appropriate.

An asterisk against a Select Committee means that it normally does not take evidence; if it does it is in private. Deliberations are always held in private. Standing Committee proceedings are normally in public.

Details of the times of sitting of these Committees and the subjects they are considering and of their membership are to be found in the House of Lords Information Bulletin and the House of Commons Information Bulletin, both published by HMSO.

HOUSE OF LORDS

SELECT COMMITTEES
  *APPELLATE COMMITTEE
  CONSOLIDATION BILLS (Joint Committee)
  EUROPEAN COMMUNITIES
    Sub-Committees:
    A. Finance, Economics and Regional Policy
    B. Trade and Treaties
    C. Education, Employment, Consumer and Social Affairs
    D. Food and Agriculture
    E. Law
    F. Energy, Transport and Research
    G. Environment
  *HOUSE OF LORDS' OFFICES COMMITTEE
    Sub-Committees:
    Administration
    Computers
    Finance
    Library

       Refreshment Department
       Staff of the House
       Works of Art
   PRIVILEGES
  *PROCEDURE
  SCIENCE AND TECHNOLOGY
  *SELECTION
  *SOUND BROADCASTING
  STATUTORY INSTRUMENTS (Joint Committee)
  UNEMPLOYMENT
STANDING COMMITTEES – Very infrequent

HOUSE OF COMMONS

SELECT COMMITTEES
  DEPARTMENTAL COMMITTEES

Name of Committee	Principal Government Departments Concerned
Agriculture	Ministry of Agriculture, Fisheries and Food
Defence	Ministry of Defence
Education, Science and Arts	Department of Education and Science
Employment	Department of Employment
Energy	Department of Energy
Environment	Department of the Environment
Foreign Affairs	Foreign and Commonwealth Office
Home Affairs	Home Office
Industry and Trade	Department of Industry, Department of Trade
Social Services	Department of Health and Social Security
Transport	Department of Transport
Treasury and Civil Service	Treasury, Civil Service Department, Board of Inland Revenue, Board of Customs and Excise
Scottish Affairs	Scottish Office
Welsh Affairs	Welsh Office

  CONSOLIDATION BILLS (Joint Committee)
  EUROPEAN LEGISLATION, etc.
  *HOUSE OF COMMONS (SERVICES)
  Sub-Committees:
     Accommodation and Administration
     Catering
     Computer

Library
STANDING COMMITTEES

Index

Abbreviations used in the index: HC (House of Commons), HL (House of Lords), HCL (House of Commons Library), HLL (House of Lords Library), EP (European Parliament), EC (European Communities)